Belgian Democracy

BELGIAN DEMOCRACY

ITS EARLY HISTORY

BY

HENRI PIRENNE

TRANSLATED BY

J. V. SAUNDERS

AMS PRESS
NEW YORK

Reprinted from the edition of 1915, Manchester
First AMS EDITION published 1970
Manufactured in the United States of America

International Standard Book Number: 0-404-05057-3

Library of Congress Card Catalog Number: 73-120219

AMS PRESS, INC.
NEW YORK, N.Y. 10003

TO MY FRIEND
PROFESSOR PAUL VINOGRADOFF
OF OXFORD.

PREFACE TO THE ENGLISH EDITION.

THIS little book first saw the light in 1910. Since that date, no work has appeared which has required me to reconsider the general ideas on which it is based. Nevertheless, this English translation includes a certain number of detailed corrections which have here and there improved the text.

The subject of this book deals with the Low Countries as a whole, using the term in its old acceptation to designate the stretch of country now comprising the French departments of the Nord and the Pas-de-Calais as well as the kingdoms of Belgium and Holland. The only democracies known to those districts before our own days were the urban democracies, and therefore no one will be surprised to find that towns are the sole topic of this little book. Moreover, the scope of the work is in practice almost entirely limited to the towns of the modern kingdom of Belgium. Nowhere in northern Europe did democratic institutions grow up with more energy and result than in the towns on the banks of the Scheldt and the Meuse. Quite apart from the historical interest which this remarkable development offers, the study of the history of democracy in the Belgium of the past is well worthy of the attention of those who wish to investigate the problems of contemporary democracy. In this relation I cannot but express my profound conviction that the vitality which the towns of Belgium have hitherto shewn in all stages of their history is a certain proof that they will assuredly renew their strength, even after the terrible disasters of which they have recently become the victims. May the English-speaking public extend to their early history a little of the sympathy which it is lavishing on their present misfortunes !

I am extremely grateful to the University of Manchester for doing this little book the honour of inclusion among the historical series of its publications. I also wish to express my indebtedness to Mr. J. V. Saunders, who undertook the task of translating this volume. The present state of affairs has made it impossible for me to take much personal share in the review of his translation, and has altogether prevented me from seeing the book in proof. I must, therefore, tender my best thanks to my friend Professor T. F. Tout, who has been good enough to make himself responsible for the revision of the translation and for seeing the work through the press; and to Miss J. M. Potter, who has given him considerable help in both these respects, and has compiled the index. To Mr. H. M. McKechnie, the secretary of the Publications Committee of the University, I must also acknowledge my obligations for much invaluable assistance.

H. PIRENNE.

GHENT,
February, 1915.

TABLE OF CONTENTS.

CHAPTER I.

THE BEGINNINGS OF THE TOWNS.

I. The Roman period and the Frankish period.—
II. Castles and Cities.—III. The Portus and
its Immigrants.—IV. The Trading Population
and its Social Demands.—V. The Guilds.

I.
The Roman Period and the Frankish Period.

Although one of the most striking characteristics of
the Low Countries is the large number of towns to be
found there, and although at all periods of their
history the townsfolk have played a leading part in
their politics, nevertheless urban life did not begin
there till comparatively late. Most of the great towns
of Italy and France, of the Rhineland and the Upper
Danube, are earlier than our era, whereas Liége,
Louvain, Mechlin, Antwerp, Brussels, Bruges, Ypres,
Ghent, Utrecht, etc., did not come into existence till
the beginning of the Middle Ages. Under the Roman
Empire Tongres was the only Netherlandish town of
note, and Tongres owed her importance to her place in
the provincial administration. When that broke down
at the time of the Germanic invasions, she lost for
ever the influence which she had for a time exercised
in her neighbourhood. In the Roman period Arlon
and Namur were only boroughs of secondary rank.

1

Tournai, though apparently more important, was so deeply affected by the Frankish conquest that the episcopal see, already established there, had to be removed to Noyon, and was not restored till the twelfth century. Thus, with very few exceptions, the Dutch and Belgian towns of our day are comparatively recent in origin. Nor is this surprising, for, situated as they were at the northern end of the Empire on the borders of the barbarian world, the basins of the Scheldt and the Meuse lay off the great trade routes and were, therefore, not readily accessible to that urban life which commercial intercourse evokes and maintains. They were crossed by a single great route running from east to west, from Cologne to Boulogne. Its branches towards the south served for the exportation of the smoke-dried meats of the country, for which there was a certain demand, and of the woollen fabrics manufactured by the peasantry of the *Morini* and *Menapii*.

The Frankish conquest wasted the provinces of *Belgica Secunda* and *Germania Inferior,* and at the same time completely altered the conditions that had until then governed the course of their history. From the establishment of the *regnum Francorum* the Rhine ceased to form the frontier of European civilization. *Belgica,* instead of lying on the circumference, as she had done in Roman times, awoke to find herself in the enjoyment of an admirable position at the centre of an extended Europe. Not only was she the meeting point of the two great nationalities (Latin and Germanic), which were to work out the civilization of the Middle Ages, but it was largely through her territory that every kind of exchange, intellectual no less than material, was effected between these peoples. After the Carolingian period her isolation was at an end, and she appeared as one of the most vigorous and prosperous countries of the West. Monasteries and great estates were covering her soil, while Charles the Great's preference for Aachen as his residence, made her the antechamber, so to speak, of the imperial palace. All who approached the sovereign from any part of Christendom, were obliged to traverse her territory. Every kind of produce necessary for the provisioning of the court was brought down her rivers; by them too the monasteries of the northern districts imported from the hills of the Moselle the wine which they could not produce under their cold and misty sky. In a Europe devoted to agriculture the Belgian province was undoubtedly able to show a comparatively well developed trade earlier than her neighbours. Quentovic (Etaples), at the mouth of the Canche; Tiel, Utrecht, and Durstede, on the lower Rhine, were the most important ports of the Carolingian monarchy in the north. Valenciennes and Maestricht, situate at the points where the old Roman road crossed the Scheldt and the Meuse, became stations for vessels and wintering places for traders. Finally the number of mints proves that the use of coin, an indisputable proof of economic progress, was steadily extending by the side of the primitive system of barter. Moreover, in spite of the paucity of our documents, we can perceive the symptoms of some industrial activity from the ninth century onwards. In the damp marshy plains of the coast, the cloth manufacture of the *Morini* and the *Menapii* revived. Their fabrics, carried to a distance by the vessels of

B

Quentovic, Tiel and Durstede, spread the fame of
" Frisian " cloaks to the foot of the Alps. Metal
working began to develop in the valley of the Meuse
at Huy and at Dinant.

The activity already displaying itself was destined
to be soon interrupted. The geographical situation of
the Low Countries, while favourable to their trade,
also exposed them to attacks from without. Here
more than anywhere else, perhaps, in this land of
estuaries wide open to the sea, heaps of smoking ruins
marked the track of the invading Normans. From
820 to 891 the country was devastated from end to
end, and, when the victory of Arnulf of Carinthia at
Louvain had at last freed it from the plunderers, its
ports no longer existed and the stations, which had
been established by the traders along its waterways,
had disappeared. Of the social progress achieved by
the close of the 9th century nothing remained.

II.

Castles and Cities.

During the anarchy of which it had just been the
victim, the country had assumed a different aspect.
The necessity of defence against the barbarians had
everywhere caused the erection of fortifications which
the documents of the period call *castra,* that is to say,
castles. Very different from the towers and keeps, in
which the barons began thenceforth to dwell, these
castra recall the ancient *acropoleis* or the *oppida* of
the Gauls and Germans. They were stone enclosures,
intended to serve as refuges for the inhabitants and
to protect against a sudden attack an abbey, a prince's

dwelling, or the central " court " of some great estate. They were very simple in plan; a rectangular curtain wall, flanked by towers and surrounded by a moat; in the interior some conventual buildings, a church, barns, dwellings for the servants of the laymen and clergy, the clergy themselves and a small military garrison (*milites castrenses*).

It was the counts who everywhere took the lead in these works of defence, for, thanks to the weakness of the royal power and the disorganization of the machinery of government, they were at that time in process of transforming themselves into territorial princes. They alone possessed the authority necessary to compel the rustic population to build the castles; they alone could direct a task which, though we cannot fill in the details, was certainly carried through with extraordinary activity.

The bishops in their turn did not rest inactive. Towards 710 the episcopal see of Tongres, which had been transferred to Maestricht in the 4th century, was set up by St. Hubert at Liége (*Leudicus vicus, Leodium*), then a small town near the Carolingian *villa* of Herstal. During the reigns of Charles the Great and Louis the Pious, the town was embellished by the prelates who dwelt there. In the middle of the 9th century there were already in course of erection two churches and a canons' minster. Bishop Hartgar (840—856) built himself a palace, much admired by his contemporaries, where he gathered round him a little band of learned men. But the Normans came, and the infant city fell a prey to the flames (881). The 10th century saw it rise again from its ruins. Richer (920—945), and then Ebrachar (959—971) rebuilt the

churches and the palace. Notger (972—1008) completed their work. Under his reign, Liége accomplished the task of surrounding herself with a strong
wall. Similar works were undertaken about the same
time at Cambrai by bishop Dodilon (888—901), at
Utrecht and at Tournai.

Throughout the 10th century then, the princes, lay
and ecclesiastical, were alike engaged in the construction of defensive enclosures. In this work the people
did not take the initiative. They allowed themselves
to be directed by their rulers and seconded their efforts
because they met the needs of the community. All
over the country there arose places of refuge and, at a
time when the need of protection was supreme, the
inhabitants of the neighbourhood came in due course
to regard these tutelary fortresses as the headquarters
of their district.

Such are the beginnings of municipal history in
the Low Countries. Obviously the needs determining
them were military. It is none the less true that the
castles of the 10th century were the ancestors of the
future towns. They not only marked the sites they
were to occupy,[1] but the organization developed within
the circuit of their walls already, in some respects,
presented features of an urban character.

The purely agricultural civilization, which prevailed
in western Europe for many centuries after the fall of
the Roman Empire, had naturally left its mark upon
the whole administration. When the towns had
disappeared, officials had no longer a fixed abode.

1. This is only completely true of the castles built by the lay
princes.   In the case of the episcopal cities the ecclesiastical
organization, by which their position was determined, must also be
taken into account.

Like the king himself, who passed incessantly from one manor to another, all officials were constantly wandering from place to place. The state had no capital; its divisions had no headquarters. The provinces (*comtés*) merely consisted of vast rural districts, constantly traversed by the counts, who dispensed justice, collected taxes, called out the military forces and in person led them into the field. It was only the centres of religious organization and of the great lay fiefs that had a permanent staff in the one case of clerks or monks, in the other of stewards, *ministeriales* and household serfs.[1] Episcopal cities, royal palaces and baronial *villae* were to be met with; but the municipal type of administration of the Roman period had vanished entirely.

Something suggesting a municipal organization began to appear again in the *castra* which sprang up in the 10th century. The territorial princes, who had built these fortresses, inevitably came to use them for the government of their lands. In them there appeared again, feebly as yet and in a very incomplete form, those fixed seats of the administrative authority which are inseparable from any advanced civilisation.

Soon the castles ceased to be mere places of refuge; the castellan, who commanded the garrison, became an official charged with the superintendence and management of the surrounding district in the prince's name. In Flanders, after the end of the 10th century, we find him endowed with judicial and financial functions in addition to his original military attributes.

The castle served also as the meeting-place for the

1. *i.e.* the serfs dwelling in their master's house as opposed to the serfs attached to the land.

échevins of the neighbourhood. In the castle at
Bruges an official house was built for their use at
a quite early date. It was in the castle again, that the
produce of the prince's demesnes round about was
stored, and that the peasants paid in kind the taxes
intended for the sustenance of the garrison. Thither
too they came at stated times to attend the general
courts, and in case of need to repair the walls or to
clean out the moat, compulsory services imposed by
the state for the maintenance of its public works.
The castle became more and more the place for the
collection of the toll levied on the wagons which went
that way, or on the boats passing along the stream
that bathed its ramparts. Finally there grew up in it
a weekly market, an indispensable means of victualling
its inhabitants.

It must not, however, be supposed that the dwellers
within these towns constituted as yet a body of
burghers, at any rate in the sense in which the word
is used in later centuries. Far from devoting themselves to the pursuit of trade or manufacture, they
were only consumers. They consisted of some dozens
of individuals, officials, soldiers and their dependents.
The object of their activities was less the castle itself
than the surrounding country. Indeed the castle only
existed for the sake of its district, of which it was the
military and administrative centre. It was a place of
business open to the people outside, who day by
day filled it with their bustling activity but did not
dwell there. Neither the peasants, who brought in the
produce of the prince's demesnes, nor the receivers and
stewards, who came to render account to the prince's
notaries, nor the *échevins,* who sat at their official

house for the administration of justice, lived within its walls. They came in from the surrounding country and thither they returned, when they had dispatched their business. The castle had ended by becoming simply a place of public resort occupied by a few permanent guards.

Such is the picture we are entitled to draw of Ghent, Bruges, Ypres, Furnes, Lille, Brussels, Louvain, Valenciennes, etc., in the 10th and 11th centuries. The episcopal cities of Utrecht, Liége and Cambrai do not present any essential differences from them. In these latter, also, the administration develops and increases in complexity, but there is still nothing that can be called a town. Nevertheless the city had an advantage over the castle by reason of its denser population and the wider sphere of its influence. The city was the scene of greater activity and traffic, and made greater demands on the neighbourhood for supplies because of the permanent residence of the bishop and his court, the increasing numbers of the clergy who served the cathedral and the other churches, the monks of the abbeys which gathered round the centre of the diocese. Steadily the needs of eccleciastical administration drew thither an increasing number of people from all points of the diocese. Add to these the litigants cited before the official, who administered justice in the bishop's court, and the masters and pupils of the schools, and we see at once the great advantages of the episcopal cities over the *castra* of the lay lords. But it was only a difference of degree. At bottom their nature was the same. Both alike recall the forts and block-houses, built by the French and the English in the

18th century, on the prairies of North America and
in the forests of Canada. Like them they were
essentially military and administrative posts.

III.
THE PORTUS AND ITS IMMIGRANTS.

This state of things could not last. With the
disappearance of the Normans and the re-establishment of security, the commercial activity, which we
noticed in the basins of the Scheldt and the Meuse in
the early part of the Carolingian period, could not but
revive. The old ports of the 9th century, Quentovic,
Tiel and Durstede, did not, it is true, rise from their
ruins. But new economic centres quickly appeared
and this time they enjoyed a lasting prosperity.
Thanks to their geographical position, commercial life
developed sooner in the Low Countries than in most
of the countries north of the Alps. They profited by
the length of their coastline, the proximity of England,
and the three deep rivers which traverse them and
connect them by natural routes, one with South
Germany and the passes giving access to Italy, the
second with Burgundy and the valley of the Saône
and the Rhône, the third with central France. All
this gave them, in the North Sea, the same part that
Venice, Pisa and Genoa played in the Adriatic and the
Mediterranean. From the 10th century onwards, they
were the meeting-point of the two great streams of
European traffic. The coasting trade of the North
Sea and the Baltic brought them into contact with the
eastern merchants, who went to and fro between the
Crimea and the Gulf of Bothnia across the plains of
Russia, and they were the natural terminus for the

Italian merchants who travelled northwards. However small the progress of international trade by the 10th century, it was more fruitful in the plains of Belgium than anywhere else.   Under its salutary influence, the rigid economic system of a purely agricultural and local life began to yield, and showed signs of growth.   The adventurous career of commerce began to attract the most enterprising of the serfs. The poor were very numerous at a time when the land alone provided the means of earning a living.   Some of them now saw a new means of getting a livelihood : they could haul a boat, or drive a wagon, or discharge a cargo.   In ever growing numbers they yielded to an attraction that increased steadily as trade developed. That attraction radiated from points naturally determined by the contour of the ground, and the direction or depth of the waterways.   These were the nodal points, if one may use the expression, of the traffic of the district.   We find them at the head of gulfs (Bruges) or where a road crosses a river (Maestricht, Valenciennes), at or near the confluence of two rivers (Liége, Mechlin, Ghent), or again at a point where a river ceases to be navigable and the boats must of necessity be unloaded (Louvain, Brussels, Douai, Ypres).   The country was dotted with trading stations. Wharves, wintering-places and halting-places soon attracted groups of men who, breaking the ties which bound them to the soil, became the unconscious artificers of social progress.

Contemporary documents give these places distinctive names.   They call them *emporia,* that is markets, or more often *portus,* a name destined to have a history.   This word had long been used to designate a place by which, thanks to the advantages of its site, merchandise regularly passed.[1] From the 10th century onwards the *portus* was no longer merely a place of call. In the Low Countries it was the first name borne by the urban aggregations. Throughout the whole of the Middle Ages the Netherlands called a town a *poort* and a burgher a *poorter*.

By a chance, at first sight strange, but which was nevertheless quite natural, it was at the foot of the castles and episcopal cities of which we were speaking just now, that the *portus* grew up in the course of the 10th century. No doubt there were exceptions to the rule. The new assemblages of traders did not mass themselves round the walls of fortresses, monasteries or episcopal sees that lay off the highways of traffic.[2] That good fortune only befel those whose situation suited the needs of trade. And that was the case with most of them. The places which lend themselves best to the defence of the country, are in fact those towards which the stream of men and goods naturally directs itself. Strategic routes are also trade routes, and the result was that, when both alike were marked out by nature, the *castra* and *portus* were coincident.

Moreover, no one felt the need for protection more severely than the traders. The shelter afforded by walled enclosures in time of war was of vital importance to men whose whole wealth consisted of moveable goods, and whom war threatened with utter ruin.

1. On this see H. Pirenne, "Villes, marchés et marchands au Moyen Age," *Revue historique* vol. lxvii (1898), p. 62; and "Les villes flamandes avant le xiie siècle," *Annales de l'Est et du Nord*, vol. i (1905), p. 22.
2. This was the case with Thérouanne which, though the seat of a bishopric, always remained a town of no importance because of the disadvantages of its position.

Further, if it sometimes happened that a *portus* was established in the open country, it was very soon removed to the neighbourhood of the nearest *castrum*. Such was no doubt the case with Lambres, near Douai, and there is no reason to suppose that this was an isolated instance.

Thus then the 10th century saw the rise of a large number of urban groups of twofold character. They arose in all parts of the Low Countries, save in the solitary and inaccessible Ardennes. In these towns two elements, entirely different in their nature, the military *castrum*, or the episcopal *cité*, stood side by side with the *portus*. In spite of local differences, the phenomenon was everywhere essentially the same. We can only say that in the episcopal cities it was a little more complex than in the mere *castra*. There, indeed, the greater extent of the walls apparently allowed the traders to take up their quarters not only outside, but, at any rate at first, even inside the enclosure.

Between the old population and the new the contrast was as striking as it could well be. The former, composed of soldiers, clerks, officials and servants were, as we have seen, consumers, and produced nothing; moreover they did not grow in numbers. The latter, continually fed by new-comers, gave itself up to the practice of trade. Instead of being dependent on supplies from outside, it maintained itself simply by its own toil. It was, in the full meaning of the word, a colony,[1] and, as in every colony, the immigrants who swelled its population, were adventurers in search of fortune, men of enterprise and activity. For the

1. Some texts of the 11th century apply the name *colonia* to Bruges and Dinant.

country-folk, the *castrum* had never been anything but a temporary refuge, the site of a weekly market or of a venerated shrine. They visited it, but they did not dwell there. The *portus,* on the other hand, retained those who came there to try a new mode of life. It was not simply an annexe to the castle, like a suburb to a town; it was differentiated by the origin of its inhabitants, by their habitual occupations and by their legal status.

The truth is that from the very beginning its population appears as a population of free men. Made up of immigrants from all parts, who had abandoned their families and the demesnes on which they had till then lived, they formed a collection of unknown men, a nameless throng, amid which the original status of each individual could not be discerned. Undoubtedly many of them were the sons of serfs, since they came from the country, and at that time servitude was the usual condition of the rural class. But who was to know it, unless they revealed it themselves? It might well happen, and indeed did happen, that some landlord of the neighbourhood, passing through the assemblage of traders, discovered one of his own men there and claimed him. But such incidents were rare. The stranger, the man from outside, had no civil status, and, having none, was treated as a free man, since there is no legal presumption of servitude. In fine the first inhabitants of the growing towns were not obliged to vindicate their claim to freedom. In virtue of the social conditions of the period it came to them of itself and without any formality. Not till much later did it become their right. It began by being a bare fact.

IV.

THE TRADING POPULATION AND ITS SOCIAL DEMANDS.

In contemporary documents the first inhabitants of the trading colonies are comprised under the name of *mercatores*. But this word must not be understood in its modern sense. The " merchants " of the early Middle Ages clearly did not constitute a specialized commercial class. They were rather a group of men engaged indifferently in buying and selling, in production and transport. The conditions existing among them differed widely. The cleverest or the most fortunate owned boats and horses, and spent the greater part of the year in distant journeys, trying their luck in the marts and either amassing, amid the varying fortunes of their perilous wanderings, a considerable fortune, or disappearing in some adventure, perishing in some obscure quarrel.[1] Others were modest pedlars, hawkers frequenting the castles or the cities round about. Others again appear as simple artisans, bakers, brewers, tanners, etc. And in a certain number of towns these artisans split into two groups at a very early date. One group was occupied in making things indispensable to the existence of the population of the place; the other worked for the

1. Bücher, *Die Entstehung der Volkswirtschaft,* 2nd edit., p. 90, and Sombart, *Der moderne Kapitalismus,* vol. i, p. 219, are undoubtedly wrong in denying the possibility of considerable fortunes during the early days of urban evolution. The sources of the period speak of " mercatores ditissimi," and even give us sufficiently precise details of the origin of the wealth of some of them. See H. Pirenne, *Villes, marchés et marchands,* pp. 64, 65. Unfortunately, the chroniclers of the period, all of them churchmen, had so little interest in commerce that we must not be astonished at not finding in them all the information we should like. It should be borne in mind that chance must have played a great part in the making of fortunes by trade.

travelling merchants who exported their products to a distance. Already, by the middle of the 11th century, the rural weavers of Flanders were flocking to the towns, and forming the first elements of that working class with which our attention will so often be occupied in the sequel. Finally we must add boatmen, free servants in the service of the merchants, and dockers, in short all the workers that traffic requires and supports.

The infant town then, the *portus,* was a permanent commercial centre. It did not owe its birth, as has sometimes been thought, to the existence of a weekly market or fair. The market and the fair were occasional; they were only due to the temporary influx of buyers and sellers from outside, who dispersed after a few hours or days. With the *portus* it was quite different; its existence depended upon an unbroken commercial activity. It grew spontaneously out of exchange between districts. Its appearance is a phenomenon analogous to that which in our times causes so many new aggregations of men at important railway junctions, and near coal-mines or petroleum springs.

The permanent seat of exchanges, the centre of a novel commercial activity in strong contrast with the stationary agricultural civilization in the midst of which it arose, the *portus* was obliged to find a form of government adapted to its needs. Markets and fairs, during the short time that they lasted, enjoyed exceptional rights and a special peace.[1] The *portus,* a perpetual fair and market, would also enjoy this special

1. See for this the valuable work of P. Huvelin, *Essai historique sur le droit des marchés et des foires.* Paris, 1897.

peace, but would enjoy it perpetually. This was all the more necessary to it because its population, composed of men who came from all parts and had been torn from their traditional environment, could not be kept in order except by a remorseless authority. Cruel punishments were indispensable to restrain their brutal instincts. The old system of fines and compositions no longer sufficed. It became necessary to proclaim a kind of martial law, and in the oldest monuments of urban law we find significant traces of the summary justice which must have held sway at first in these communities of traders.[1]

It was the same with civil as with criminal law. How could the trading group exist and develop under the dominion of stereotyped customs which had till then sufficed for an entirely rural population? The clumsy and complicated procedure, the ancient forms of mortgage, loan and distraint, were replaced by something simpler and more rapid. The daily pursuit of commerce elaborated a new custom, the *jus mercatorum*, which of necessity reacted on the old territorial customs, and, inside the *portus*, gradually modified their character. Severe repression in criminal cases, rapid procedure in civil disputes—these were the elementary needs of the urban population, and these were also its earliest demands.

Other needs and other demands were provoked by, and kept pace with, them. To begin with, the change of law entailed a corresponding change in the judiciary. It is evident that the old courts of the *échevins* of the Carolingian times, drawn from the country side and meeting periodically within the walls

1. Compare the exactly analogous lynch law in America to-day.

of the castle, could no longer serve to administer the custom of the *portus*. It therefore became necessary to create a special court of justice, the members of which could only be chosen from among the inhabitants. The financial administration too required remodelling no less than the administration of justice. The needs of trade could not be met by a system elaborated to suit a purely rural economy and adapted to a time when produce rather than money was the medium of exchange. Arbitrary taxation and remorseless exactions of market-tolls became intolerable in the trading world. The growth of movable property burst the bonds of fiscal institutions adapted to a time when land was the only form of wealth. Here too the need of reform made itself imperiously felt.

Finally the personal status of the individual had also to be adjusted to the conditions under which the trading population lived. The settlers within the *portus*, for the most part young unmarried men, were obliged to take their wives from the neighbouring country or from the castle. But in the country and in the castle the normal status of the people was servile. The men of the *portus* were compelled, then, to marry serfs. What was to happen if the lord of the land, applying his traditional rights in all their rigour, claimed the children they brought into the world?[1] It is certain that no one up to that time had protested against the custom by which the issue of two un-free parents was divided between their respective over-lords. Outrageous as it seems to us, it was a very natural custom under the circumstances.

1. Of course the status of the child followed that of the mother : "partus ventrem sequitur."

The serfs of an estate married the serfs of the neighbouring estate, and the division of the children was in
fact only the division of their labour and did not break
up the family. But what had been tolerable in the
servile circumstances of country life, ceased to be so
in the town. To the peasant it was not an intolerable
hardship that the law of the estate under which he
lived, should extend to his offspring. For the trader,
the very thought of such an interference must have
seemed monstrous and unendurable. He required
that upon marriage his wife should become free, like
himself, and that his children should be free-born. In
the end custom had to give way before the new
social units which were springing up in the bosom
of the nation, because it was no longer applicable.

Thus a long train of social changes was destined
to follow from the simple fact of the appearance of
groups of traders under the walls of the castles.
Under the pressure of necessity a complete programme
of reforms emerged. It was quite undesigned; without any preconceived theory or any inspiring ideal,
the new needs demanded satisfaction. They tended
to overthrow utterly the law and the administration of
the period. Never perhaps, except at the end of the
18th century and in our own times, has civilization
had to face such a thorough reconstruction. Never
has it been so deeply and so directly affected by
economic conditions.

V.

THE GUILDS.

To understand how urban law triumphed—and triumphed so easily—it is necessary to bear in mind two circumstances which favoured its progress : first, the plasticity of all institutions at the period of its birth, and, secondly, the liberty which the authorities allowed it at the beginning. A customary law, unwritten, traditional and rudimentary, and an administration, patriarchal in form and worked by hereditary officials, could not be permanently imposed on the new manifestations of social activity, which appeared along with the revival of commerce. The princes, for their part, had no thought of trammelling a movement which, far from menacing them, turned rather to their advantage, since it increased their resources as the growth of traffic rendered their market-dues more productive. All, laymen and ecclesiastics alike, hastened to take under their protection the traders passing through their territory. From the beginning of the 11th century, the peace of God and the peace of king or count, put them under the protection of the church, or of the sources of seignorial justice.

On the other hand, in the territories of lay princes we do not find that the state interfered in the organization of the trading colonies. During the whole of the 10th century and the greater part of the 11th it ignored them. It took no notice of the differences that distinguished them sharply from the rest of the population of the district. It did not in any way modify its principles of administration in their favour. Without any regard for their economic position and their concomitant needs, it exacted the same payments, the same services, and the same imposts, as from the other inhabitants of the castelry or district. Incapable of adapting itself to, or of answering to, the necessities of a life like theirs, it charged a high price for the protection it afforded them, and its authority only made itself felt by a series of exactions and abuses. But if it harassed them, it did not suppress them. It did not give them any institutions of their own, but it did not hinder them from providing them for themselves. The principle of authority, under which the castles had been built, gave place in the *portus* to the principle of self-government. From the beginning it was freedom that nourished the life of the town. It was the principle of association that made good the deficiencies of the official representatives of the power of the state, and gradually elaborated the machinery, the means, and the methods of government most indispensable to it.

We do not know, and we shall never know, much about the activity of the early towns during the early period of beginnings and experiments. The historical writings of the time, composed by the clergy and mindful only of the deeds of princes and bishops, paid no heed to the obscure immigrants who were paving the way for a future of which they themselves could not foresee the greatness.[1] In order to get a picture of their primitive organization, we have to seek laboriously for traces of it in documents of a later

---

1. Giles of Orval, for instance, quoting a passage from the charter granted to the men of Huy in 1066, by the bishop of Liége, omits the rest of it so as not to weary the reader.

date. There is evidence enough to prove that settled government first arose among them through the operation of the principle of free association. For these new-comers, these waifs unknown to one another, it was the representative of, or substitute for, the organization of the family. Side by side with the patriarchal institutions, which had till then held sway, there arose under its influence a social unit of a novel form, which was more artificial but at the same time simpler.

It is true that the principle of association is much older than urban life. We know that there existed in Frankish times guilds that were earlier than the beginnings of Christianity. But these primitive guilds do not appear to have had any political character. They were simple fellowships whose members lent aid to one another and met together to drink. Their religious character, pagan at first, but subsequently Christian, was strongly marked. In the towns the guilds were now much more than this, for the development of trade entirely transformed the institution. Essentially travellers, merchants could not venture abroad alone without running the risk of forthwith falling a prey to some robber. They were therefore compelled to form regular caravans in order to make their long journeys with safety. In each town they assembled before their departure under the command of a chief, (*Hansgraf, comes mercatorum, cuens des marchands*). At their head marched a standard-bearer (*schildrake*), behind whom stretched the train of wagons and beasts of burden. To the packages and bales were bound the tents and tent-poles that were to be set up for the camp at night, as

well as the weapons, bows, arrows and swords, to
which the comrades would have recourse at the first
alarm.[1] Naturally such an organization implied
rigorous and practically military discipline. Like the
modern caravans in the East, these mediæval caravans
obeyed regulations, which laid down not only their
order of march, but also each man's position and
rights at the markets and fairs where they stopped.
The dangers they ran together, the obedience rendered
to the same chief, the community of interest and
sentiment, maintained among their members a powerful corporate spirit. When it returned home the
association was not dissolved. It became a guild, a
hansa, a brotherhood, a *carité.* From the 11th century
we find the guild of Saint-Omer fully organized, and
the statutes of the Cloth Hall at Valenciennes prove
that the *carité* of that town is equally ancient.

Now these phenomena were certainly not isolated.
Probability compels us to admit that, as like causes
produce like effects, all the places devoted to external
trade learnt to develop similar institutions. In spite
of differences of detail and diversities of name, each
must have had its association of merchants, more or
less numerous and more or less powerful. As at
Saint-Omer, each of these associations no doubt had
its place of meeting and its elders, called its members
brethren, and exercised over them a certain corporate
jurisdiction. An extraordinary fact, which testifies to
the rapid progress society was making, is that some of

1. I borrow these details from the statutes of the Cloth Hall
at Valenciennes, Caffiaux, *Memoires de la Société des antiquaires
de France,* vol. xxxviii (1877), and from the bye-laws of the Hansa
of London. See H. Pirenne, "La hanse flamande de Londres,"
Bull. de l'Academie de Belgique, Classe des Lettres, 1899.

them had a notary or a chancellor charged with the duty of keeping their records; he may be considered as the distant ancestor of the later town clerk.[1]

But that was not the whole extent of the activities of the guilds and the *carités*. They did not content themselves with their corporate powers. They boldly assumed public functions, and since the political authorities remained inactive, they acted instead of them. At Saint-Omer the guild set aside each year the balance of its revenues for the common good, that is for the maintenance of the roads, the construction of the gates and the fortifications of the town. Other documentary evidence justifies the inference that much the same thing happened at Arras, Lille and Tournai at a very early date. Indeed, by the 13th century, we find the finances of the town placed under the control of the *charité Saint-Christophe* at Tournai and of the Count of the Hansa at Lille.[2]

There is enough evidence to justify the assertion made above, and to prove that it was the association of traders that first introduced some order and stability among the mixed and often, no doubt, discordant elements, of the population in the Flemish and Walloon *portus*. Officially the guild had no right to act as it did; its interference is explicable solely on the ground of the cohesion of its members and the influence enjoyed by their group. For in the urban aggregations of the 11th century the travelling merchants evidently formed an upper class. Among them were found the most energetic and the most

1. G. Espinas and H. Pirenne, "Les coutumes de la gilde marchande de Saint-Omer," in *Le Moyen Age*, 1901, p. 189.
2. See L. Verriest, "Qu'était la charité Saint-Christophe à Tournai, *Bull. de la Comm. royale d'histoire de Belgique*, 1908, p. 139.

enterprising; among them too appeared the first men of wealth. The guild not only laid the foundations of the urban constitution, but also, among the crowd of immigrants who had come in from the country, it was the starting point for the formation of different social classes determined by differences of fortune. The richest men naturally took the lead and played the most active part in the trading colonies, just as in the open country the possession of land conferred upon the great landowners superior rank and imposed upon them greater responsibilities. The aristocratic character of rural institutions in the Frankish period, and the aristocratic character which was soon to mark urban administration, are explicable by the rapid concentration of capital, whether consisting of land or of movable property, in the hands of a few privileged persons.

But the wealth of the merchants was beneficial to the commonwealth, and their use of it justified the influence they enjoyed. The initiative of the corporations was rivalled by that of individuals. Alongside the works of public utility supported by the guilds, we know of others dating from the 11th century that were due to private persons. Certain rich merchants employed their wealth liberally in the service of their fellow citizens. In 1043 one of them built a church at Saint-Omer;[1] a little later at Cambrai another bought up the toll of one of the town gates and provided for the maintenance of a bridge.[2]

Thus, quite soon in the history of the *portus*, we can perceive the first traces of the urban patriciate.

1. Giry, *Histoire de Saint-Omer*, p. 370.
2. *Gestes des évêques de Cambrai*, edited by De Smedt, p 131.

A wealthy class grew up which undertook the direction of the community. Influential owing to its social importance and powerful by reason of the close association of its members in a single body, this class launched into politics. The demand of the burgesses, whose programme we have already tried to sketch, found in the young patriciate at once their weapon and their champion.

CHAPTER II.

THE GROWTH OF URBAN INSTITUTIONS.

I. THE PRINCES, LAY AND ECCLESIASTICAL. THE COM-
MUNE OF CAMBRAI. THE FLEMISH TOWNS.—
II. DEVELOPMENT OF URBAN LAW. THE RIGHTS
OF PERSONS AND STATUS OF LAND IN THE TOWNS.
III. THE TOWN COURT. THE ÉCHEVINS. THE
COUNCIL. THE JURATI.

I.

THE PRINCES, LAY AND ECCLESIASTICAL. THE COM-
MUNE OF CAMBRAI. THE FLEMISH TOWNS.

Until about the middle of the 11th century the princes, as we have already seen, did not concern themselves with the trading colonies. Left to themselves, the latter set up a rudimentary state, existing *de facto*, though lacking both legal sanction and serious guarantee of permanence. For its conversion into a state existing *de jure*, for the transformation of the *portus* into a town, and of its inhabitants into burghers, and finally, for the official ratification of its autonomy, and for the growth of the institutions necessary to complete it, the intervention of the sovereign power was necessary. It was, moreover, inevitable, since the growing intensity of urban life was sure to attract the attention of the princes, and thereafter their relations with the towns were bound to become more numerous and more complicated.

In the Low Countries the lay princes were on the whole more sympathetic towards the towns than were the ecclesiastical princes. The reason is easily comprehensible. The counts of Flanders, of Hainault and of Holland, like all the other potentates of the Middle Ages, were always on the move. They had no fixed residence and, with their little courts, were continually wandering from one part of their lands to another. Thus they were not in permanent contact with the urban population and rarely came into conflict with it. Up to the 12th century their attitude towards the towns was generally friendly. The towns for their part were careful not to annoy a power which, while protecting them against the petty local lords, their troublesome and dangerous neighbours, abstained from interfering in their affairs.

The bishops found themselves in quite a different position. With their permanent homes in their cities, they were compelled to enter into daily relations with the inhabitants, and to interest themselves in their acts and deeds. Further, being more civilized than the laymen, they had a theory of government. It was based on the twin principle of obedience to the spiritual and to the temporal power, both emanating from God Himself. At Liége, Utrecht and Cambrai, the able prelates, who were charged by the emperors with the administration of those dioceses, strove, during the whole of the 10th and 11th centuries, to maintain loyalty to the sovereign and the *disciplina teutonica*.[1] It is quite clear that the organization of feudal institutions in their territories had reached a

1. See H. Pirenne, *Histoire de Belgique*, vol. i, 3rd ed., p. 65.

high level, and that the condition of the peasants, under their strong and watchful authority, was singularly favourable. The petty nobles of the district found obedience less easy, and it was they, no doubt, who, at Liége under bishop Ebrachar (959—971), and at Cambrai under bishop Engran (956—960), provoked risings about which we have hardly any detailed information.[1]

On the other hand it is certain that the bishops' cities, along with a larger population and a busier life than was to be found in the castles of the lay princes, enjoyed also a more stable order and a stronger police. The bishops took every means in their power to ensure the food supply, superintend the market and build walls and bridges. Notger of Liége (972—1018) diverted an arm of the Meuse to improve the health of the town, and to secure the whole of it from attack.

But it was exactly the activity and care which the bishops displayed on behalf of their subjects, that brought about the collisions between them. The immigration of the traders in the course of the 10th century complicated the situation because it produced new needs, and aroused demands till then unknown. Now, in the very city where they themselves dwelt,[2] the prelates could not without risk allow the traders that autonomy which they enjoyed under the lay princes. They naturally wished to subject them to their own unlimited paternal rule. Having little sym-

1. An attempt has been made to treat these disturbances as attempts towards forming a commune, but without any justification.
2. I limit my remark to the cities which were themselves episcopal sees. We find that the lesser towns of the episcopal principalities did not have to strive against their bishops. In the principality of Liége, Huy obtained a charter of liberties in 1066.

pathy with commerce, the church, moreover, drew no
distinction between usury and the operations to which
commerce gave rise. She taxed with the sin of *avaritia*
the tendency to the steady accumulation of wealth
which modern economists call capitalism. Hence
arose misunderstandings, the clashing of interests and
presently a hostility which only awaited an opportunity to break out.[1]

The opportunity presented itself at the time of the
Investiture contest. The traders, dissatisfied with
their imperialist bishops, embraced the pope's cause
with enthusiasm. Religious and political antagonism
marched abreast. The priests, who stirred up the
people against the simoniacal prelates, nowhere found
warmer support than among the traders and the
artisans, whose economic demands were suddenly
discovered to be agreeable to the good cause.[2] The
history of Cambrai proves this with great clearness.
During the 11th century the prosperity of that town
had grown immensely. At the foot of the primitive
city there was grouped a commercial suburb which
had been fortified in 1070. But the trading population, placed under the administration of the bishop's

1. For the attitude of the clergy towards commerce, see, for
example, "Vita Sancti Guidonis" (*Bollandist Acta Sanctorum*,
Sept., vol. iv, p. 43): "Mercatura raro aut nunquam ab aliquo diu
sine crimine exerceri potuit."

2. The events that took place in the Low Countries at this date
should be compared with those which happened in the Rhine and
Lombard towns at the same time. It should not be forgotten that
the support, given to the pope by feudalists during the Investiture
contest, is to a large extent explicable by their interests. Gregory
VII had on his side the two forces in the empire which were going
to dominate the future, the lay princes and the towns. The emperor
was only supported by the partisans of a society in the act of
disappearing. There is here a whole group of phenomena in general
too little heeded by the students of this great conflict.

castellan and officers, endured their authority with
impatience. For a considerable time they had been
secretly preparing for revolt, when, in 1077, the
bishop Gerard II had to absent himself in order
to receive his investiture at the hands of the emperor.
Scarcely had he started, when the people, led by the
richest traders of the town, rose in revolt, gained
possession of the gates and proclaimed a commune.
The poor, the artisans, above all the weavers, supported the movement the more vigorously because, in
his sermons, the Hildebrandine priest, Ramihrdus,
denounced the bishop as a simoniac, and roused in
their hearts that popular mysticism which, at a later
date, we shall so often find accompanying the
upheavals of urban democracy. The citizens swore to
maintain the commune amid general enthusiasm, some
favouring it for very practical reasons, others from
religious fervour. Essentially revolutionary, the commune aimed at destroying, at one stroke, a rule that
interest and faith rendered doubly odious. When we
contemplate the traders, the weavers and Ramihrdus
working together, we cannot but be reminded of the
city of Florence, at once commercial, mechanical and
mystic, of the time of Savonarola.

The need of upholding by force the new rule, which
they had established for themselves, drove all the
inhabitants, great and small, into a close union. Here
there could be no question of leaving the lead to a
guild. In view of the certain return of the bishop,
a measure to secure the public safety was imperatively
necessary. Such was the commune, sworn to by all
and binding upon all. It is indeed quite clear that the
commune of Cambrai was essentially military. Its

organization was adapted to conflict, and it is highly
significant that it was an episcopal city, which first
saw the birth of an instrument of economic enfran-
chisement that so many cities of Germany and
Northern France were to appropriate in due course.

We have much less information about the history
of the burgher body at Liége than at Cambrai. Texts
of the beginning of the 12th century enable us to
gather that it had made inroads on the jurisdiction of
the canons of the cathedral, since, in 1107, the emperor
Henry V. was asked to confirm the privileges of the
latter. Of Utrecht we know even less. We may,
however, be sure that the population of that city did
not fail to take advantage of the struggle which broke
out in 1122 between their bishop Godebold and the
emperor Henry V. It is impossible to say whether
it was in consequence of that event that they obtained
from the bishop a " privilege," which was ratified by
Henry. In any case it is very interesting to be assured
that the traders played the leading part at Utrecht as
in Flanders and at Cambrai. Of this there can be
no doubt, when we find the emperor modifying the
rate of the market dues, on the demand of the *hones-
tiores cives,* in order to gain the support of the town.[1]
At Tournai, to which the bishop's see was only
restored in 1146 after its removal to Noyon at the
beginning of the Frankish period, our sources make
no mention of any conflict, and we are entitled to
suppose that the beginnings of town organization
were made as peacefully as in Flanders. In Flanders
there was no hostility between the counts and the

1. Waitz, *Urkunden zur Deutschen Verfassungsgeschichte,* 1871,
p. 28.

burghers. Not only did the prince leave them to work out their own salvation, but, as early as the second half of the 11th century, we find him intervening in their favour. It follows that from that time they were powerful enough for their sympathy to be worth winning. Robert the Frisian (1071—1093), who came to power by usurpation, clearly tried to attach them to his side. His successors, Robert of Jerusalem (1093—1111) and Baldwin VII. (1111—1119), pursued, in dealing with the burghers, the policy which they had inherited from its author. Under the reign of these princes, formal concessions established for the first time on a legal footing a special status for the urban population. They received privileges in the matter of market dues, of military service, of jurisdiction and procedure. From the outset of the 12th century, all Flanders from Arras to Bruges was dotted with active and flourishing towns, relying on the protection of the prince and acknowledging his benefits by their unswerving fidelity. In 1127 when Charles the Good was assassinated, they rose unanimously to avenge him, and the loyalty, which made them take up their arms, provoked also their first interference in the politics of the county. They claimed a voice in the choice of the new prince. They dictated their conditions to William of Normandy without troubling themselves about the orders of the king of France; they rose against him when he broke his promises, and it was they who established on the throne a new dynasty in the person of Thierry of Alsace (1128).

II.

DEVELOPMENT OF URBAN LAW. THE RIGHTS OF PERSONS AND STATUS OF LAND IN THE TOWNS.

Whether they fought with their princes or lived on good terms with them, the towns sooner or later, at the end of the 11th or the beginning of the 12th century, achieved their aim. Henceforth they constituted corporate persons. Their population was no longer a simple group of human beings, recognizable by its social characteristics. It enjoyed its own law : it had become a class with a legal status. The burghers, like the nobles, obtained legal recognition. For the latter the profession of arms, for the former the profession of trade and industry, had in the long run won the official recognition of a privileged position. It is of importance to analyse burgher privilege and to become familiar with its specific characteristics.

These characteristics, it must be admitted, are by no means peculiar to the Low Countries. The growth of municipal government has been in its essential features the same in the different parts of Europe. It was in no way a national phenomenon. The drama of the economic changes that gave rise to it, displayed in its course vicissitudes differing in detail; but the thread of the story is the same everywhere. Like feudalism, the town constitutions are the result of social conditions independent of race, language or frontiers. No doubt the individual differences were innumerable but they must not mislead us. If we look closely, we see that there exist " families " of towns, but we notice also that these families spread indifferently on both sides of the frontiers marked on the map of Europe.

They are not determined by either ethnography or politics. Cologne, Mainz and Worms are more closely related to Reims, Noyon, Laon and Cambrai than to Magdeburg or to Lübeck; Lille and Arras, whose population is purely Latin, are the sisters of Ghent and Bruges, whose population is just as purely Germanic; and conversely, there is more affinity between Liége and Utrecht, than between Utrecht and Amsterdam. Special circumstances such as the geographical situation, the particular nature of the trade or industry carried on in each of them, or their relations with their princes, stamped on their evolution the traits that distinguish the towns in different regions. But the diversity they display does not proceed from a diversity of nature. Everywhere the starting point must be sought in economic causes, of which the burgess body was, after all, only a result. The more active these causes were, the more obvious is their influence. The less their development has been hampered, the more the municipal constitutions are seen in their purest and, if the expression be allowed, their most classic form. Now this was particularly the case in the Low Countries and above all in Flanders. More actively devoted to trade and industry than the other countries lying to the north of the Alps, this region allows us to study the birth and development of civic institutions, under peculiarly favourable circumstances. Municipal life manifested itself more energetically and in greater purity here than anywhere else, and it is in this country, lying between the two great civilizations of the West, open to all their influences, and itself divided between the Latin and Germanic races, that we can form the best idea, thanks

D

to the variety and the richness of the soil in which it
sprang up, of the true nature of the mediæval town.

Its most striking characteristic is that it is based on
privilege. Like the noble, the burgher was a privileged person, and therein lay the clearest distinction
between the town of the Middle Ages and the town
of antiquity. In antiquity the city was the centre of
the whole life of the people who built it. There they
had their temples and their magistrates; there they
met at fixed seasons to take part in elections or
religious festivals. However much the peasant
differed from the inmate of the city in his way of life,
he had the same right to the title of " citizen." The
jus civitatis was not the law of a class; it belonged to
all the free men of the state whether they dwelt
inside or outside the walls. The word *civitas* did not
signify the city strictly so called, the mass of buildings
surrounded by walls; it was applicable to the whole
of the territory of which the city was the heart and
the brain.

The mediæval city, on the other hand, constituted
a legal unit distinct from the surrounding country.
Its gates once passed, a man escaped from territorial
law and came under an exceptional jurisdiction.
Between the countryman and the burgher there was
neither community of interest nor community of civil
status. Each lived under his own form of government, had his own magistrates and ruled or was ruled
on different principles. The ordinary system of law,
which had continued to control the country, no longer
applied to the town. It formed a legal island, a real
" immunity," in the midst of the plain which the eye
took in from the top of the municipal belfry.

To begin with, the town cut itself off from the countryside by its walls. For since the beginning of the 12th century, the group of traders which had clustered round the primitive castle, had completed its defensive works. Encircled by a wall or a ditch, it had in its turn become a fortress. What was to begin with an open suburb (*foris burgus*) was now a borough-(*bourg*); so much so, that thenceforth its inhabitants took the name of burghers (*burgenses*).[1] From that moment the old *castrum,* which still rose in the centre of the town, ceased to be of any further use. Built as a place of refuge for the neighbouring country folk, it had survived its usefulness when it found itself imprisoned by the surrounding houses. Its walls, no longer of service, were not kept up; they fell into ruins or were demolished. Indeed it often happened that, as at Ghent for example, or at Valenciennes, the princes granted the very site, on which it stood, to the town, as building land. In short, of the two elements, side by side at the beginning, the military *castrum* and the trading *portus,* the latter absorbed the former, and it is strictly true to say that, at any rate in the Low Countries, it was not the *bourg* but the *faubourg,* not the fortress but the suburb, that constituted the town.

But if it caused the disappearance of the castles of

---

1. The first mention of this word in Flanders occurs in 1056 at Saint-Omer. It evidently comes from France where it had already been long in use. Nevertheless, as we have seen above, the language of the Netherlands preserved by its side the old name of *poorter.* From Flanders the word *burgensis* spread over the rest of Belgium; we find it at Huy in 1066. Then from Belgium it reached Germany. It is a phenomenon very curious and significant for the appreciation of mediæval town life, that the commonest name for the essentially peaceful municipal population should be of military origin.

refuge, the town itself became their substitute. It rendered the rural population the service which the castles had formerly rendered to the countryfolk. Its ramparts were now to shelter the peasants in time of war. For centuries they were, at the approach of the enemy, to crowd its streets and its market places with their cattle and their wagons. Thus the fortified town served a double purpose. It enclosed the municipal community and in time of danger threw open its gates to the people outside. It was thus a place of refuge for the neighbourhood, and the burghers, who had built their walls at their own expense, found in the security they offered to the peasants, the justification for their own privileged position and for the subjection in which they held the country people.

Without their walls, however, the burghers could not defend either their property or their institutions, exposed as they were to all attacks, and defenceless against greed. The need of defence was more impera-tively felt by them than by any other class of society. The clergy were protected by the reverence in which they were held; the nobles and the peasants, living by the land, "which the enemy cannot carry away,"[1] were always sure of being able to repair their losses after pillage or invasion. But the more complex economic life of the civic communities demanded instruments more numerous, more delicate and, above all, more costly, than those needed in the country side. The very existence of the towns was only maintained by the exercise of various callings requiring all kinds of equipment. To such a society pillage and invasion

1. The words of Count Baldwin V of Hainault in Gislebert, *Chronicon Hanoniense,* p. 174 (ed. Vanderkindere).

were terrible calamities. Hence the protecting wall was a prime necessity. Not only were no towns unwalled, but also in the budget of each town the military expenses were far in excess of all others together. More than that, it seems clear that the first taxes levied upon the town were destined to no other purpose than the upkeep and construction of the walls. The fines inflicted by the town court were often appropriated *ad opus castri,* and at Liége the *accise* of the commune continued to bear the significant name of *fermeté*[1] till the end of the Middle Ages. Within the circuit of peace[2] enclosing the town, there reigned also a law of peace. By this we must understand a particularly severe penal law, intended to maintain public order by the fear of pitiless expiations. All the most ancient documents of this municipal law are full of corporal punishments : hanging, beheading, castration, maiming. It applied the *lex talionis* in all its rigour : an eye for an eye, a tooth for a tooth. *Secundum quantitatem facti punietur,* says the charter of Saint-Omer, *scilicet oculum pro oculo, dentem pro dente, caput pro capite reddet.*

It was not only in vigorous repression of crime, but much more in respect of civil status, that the law of the town was distinguished from that of the open country. Here the procedure was simpler and quicker, and the methods of legal proof were greatly improved. From the old primitive custom sprang a new custom, adapted to the needs created by commercial and industrial life.

1. *Fermeté,* in Latin *firmitas,* means fortification. It survives in the numerous towns called La Ferté in modern France.
2. The chronicler Galbert at the beginning of the 12th century calls the towns *loci pacifici* and contrasts them with *forinseci loci.*

We are almost entirely in the dark about the whole of this law, because it was called into existence by the practical necessities that arose day by day, and it grew independently of, and parallel to, the charters granted by the princes. Further, it was rapidly modified by the active life that attended its birth, and shaped its development in accordance with its own incessant movements. It was a law " from day to day," to use the phrase of the documents.[1] Unwritten until the middle of the 13th century, it then began to be recorded in the " bans," or the *vorboden*, of the *échevins*. The legal innovations made by the towns were not confined to procedure, civil law, commercial law and the penal code. They appeared still more clearly in all that concerned the rights of persons and the status of land.

We have seen that at the beginning two populations, that of the *castrum* and that of the *portus*, lived side by side. The first, and the more ancient, consisted of knights and *ministeriales*,[2] of clergy and serfs. The second class was treated as free in consequence of the difficulty of ascertaining the condition of its members. In course of time, and under the influence of the causes of which we have spoken, the freedom of the immigrants into the *portus* was extended to the old inhabitants of the *castrum*. The commercial suburb not only absorbed the military borough, it also communicated to it its legal status. Either as the result of mixed marriages, or by the entry

1. William of Normandy, in 1127, permits the burghers of Flanders " ut de die in diem consuetudinarias leges suas corrigerent."
2. This word is applied to men who, while not of free birth, were employed by their lord in administration or in war, and were thus gradually blended with the knightly class.

of the serfs into commercial occupations, servitude disappeared and, on the whole, disappeared very quickly. At the same time the knights deserted their old fortresses, which were now useless. In the course of the 12th century almost all of them abandoned the town to the burghers and withdrew into the country. We no longer find them except in the episcopal cities, where a certain number were still retained by the presence of the bishop. But in the lay principalities, in Hainault, in Flanders, in Brabant and in Holland, almost all the knights gave up living in towns where they could only continue to reside by submitting to the municipal law.

The clergy naturally stayed, and it may fairly be asserted that from the 12th to the 16th century they were the only non-burghers residing in the towns. According to circumstances their relations with the town population differed considerably. At the bishops' sees, where they were very numerous and very wealthy, and where their interests often conflicted with those of the burghers, there was much quarrelling between the two elements. For instance at Liége, the cathedral canons, gathering round them the chapters of the seven collegiate churches, possessed a power which for a long time hindered the complete development of the commune. In Flanders, on the other hand, where the civil population was in the ascendant, the clergy did not attempt resistance. The monasteries were content with their immunities, and watched with composure the active application of the municipal regulations. As for the secular clergy, almost entirely composed of parish priests, habitually recruited among the burghers, and sometimes nominated by them to their cures, they never possessed either the power or, for that matter, the desire to oppose them. The bishops of Tournai tried hard to interfere in the Flemish towns in favour of the clergy : but their attempts, to which we shall return later, failed completely and they had the wisdom not to persist. Thus then, with the exception of the churchmen who lived under the canon law, the whole population of the towns shared the same law, and shared it because all those who dwelt within the circle of the town walls were alike in the enjoyment of freedom.

Freedom, which had become so rare in the course of the 11th century that the word free was a synonym for noble, was thenceforth the legal status of the burgher. " The air of the town gives freedom," said the mediæval proverb, and it was strictly true. In modern times the slave who sets foot on the soil of a European state is a free man. In the same way, after the 12th century, the villein, who had spent a year and a day in a town, found himself emancipated. There might be, and there were, striking social contrasts among the burghers. But there no longer existed differences in the eye of the law. The poorest artisan and the richest merchant were alike inhabitants of the town and alike free. Thenceforth it was, so to speak, their natural privilege and perhaps the most striking mark of their caste. In 1335 the *échevins* of Ypres replied with pride to those of Saint-Dizier that they had " never heard of men of servile status." [1]

Freedom of the soil in the town kept pace with personal freedom. Here again we find ourselves face

1. "Omques n'avons oy de gens de serve condicion," Beugnot, *Les Olim*, vol. ii, p. 770.

to face with a necessary result of the burghers' social activity. Before the trading groups were formed, the land was only valuable for farming purposes. The houses upon it were simply constituent parts of the domain. The peasant's dwelling was a mere appendage of the *mansus* or allotment, the unit of labour, and was indissolubly attached to it. The one was transferred with the other, whether by inheritance, sale or gift. But in the town, where there was concentrated a population not bound to the soil, a quite different state of affairs necessarily grew up. To the burgher, living by commerce or subsisting by the practice of a trade, his house was the essential thing. A dwelling wherein to shelter himself and to practise his calling was his one need. In his eyes the house was only a piece of furniture, independent of the land on which it stood.[1] What was originally an accessory was now the chief thing, and at the same time its site was destined to a new purpose, and acquired an unsuspected value, in becoming building land (*mansionaria terra*). The owners of the soil hastened to profit by the situation. They divided their ground into sections, which they granted to the immigrants into the *portus* on condition that they paid a rent. Further, they took care to assess the rent at a moderate rate to attract new comers. Want of information prevents us from filling in the details of the process of town settlement. But later documents permit us to discern the chief features. Whether the growing towns were planted on the domain of a prince, a

1. It is well known that the oldest sources for town law do actually regard houses as moveable property, and often consider the case of the removal of a house from one town to another.

monastery or a baron, whether the land that town houses were to cover was virgin soil or tilled land, everywhere its holders saw only a *substratum* for building. They did not try to retain it in its old feudal category. The burghers replaced the "manses" and " cultures," which had till then borne the burden of contributions of forced labour,[1] by lines of houses, each surrounded by a *pourpris*, a court or vegetable garden.

At once these houses proved to be a more valuable property than their site. The ease with which they could be let, assured for their owners abundant and regular profits. Soon, by the side of the land assessment, fixed once and for all on each parcel of land that was built upon, new charges, to which the name of rents was generally given, were levied on the house itself. Here the town's credit was first brought into play. The house served in the first instance as a pledge guaranteeing the payment of the ground rent to the owner of the soil. But with the increasing prosperity of the towns, and the consequent rapid depreciation in the purchasing power of money, the value of the house rose so high that the payment of the ground rent was only a subordinate expense. Now the landlord's right did not extend beyond the demand for this original charge. It was therefore lawful for the owners of the houses to burden them with new rent charges. If they wished to obtain ready money, they

1. At Ghent the names of a square in the town (*couter, i.e. cultura*), and of one of the oldest streets (*neder couter*), recall to this day of existence of the " cultures " of the monastery of St. Peter. For all that concerns the land in the towns see G. Des Marez, *Histoire de la propriété foncière dans les villes du Moyen Age et specialement en Flandre*. Gand, 1898.

gave a mortgage, that is to say, they engaged to make an annual payment of interest, with the house as security. The converse operation, the taking up of a mortgage, was in turn, for the traders who amassed money, the safest means of investing their profits. Everywhere the house, the permanent source of income and the essential basis of credit, caused the soil on which it stood, to be, one might almost say, forgotten. It only brought in an annual sum of less and less account as the value of money continued to fall. After the 13th century, the descendants of the ground landlords of the original building land found that they had been in effect despoiled, for the benefit of the descendants of those who had built the houses. Nothing remained to them of their property but the right to a very small ground rent, and to certain payments when the site changed hands. Each of the holders of land possessed a landbook, a " terrier " (*cynsbock*), where these transfers were recorded in the presence of witnesses who formed the land court (*laethof*) of the lord of the soil. He was thus in reality no longer anything but a sort of registrar.[1]

III.

The Town Court. The *Échevins*. The Council. The *Jurati*.

The whole of the body of law, real, personal, penal, civil and commercial, which was the product of civic conditions, would have been ineffective unless there

---

1. The history of landed property in the towns of the Middle Ages seems to me to have developed on the whole in the same way as in England, where theoretically the king remained owner of the land. But this theoretical ownership in no way hindered the spread and free play of effective ownership.

had existed a tribunal to put it into force. In the plastic society of the Middle Ages, each class of men lived according to its own custom and under its special jurisdiction. Outside the judicial organization of the state, the church had its ecclesiastical courts, the nobility its feudal courts, and the peasants their manorial courts. The burghers in their turn obtained their *échevins'* courts. Thus each town secured some sort of immunity at a period which cannot be determined with precision, but which must have begun in the second half of the 11th century.

Between the immunity of the town and the ancient immunity of the Frankish period, the differences were always numerous and significant. The immunity of the Franks was a privilege by which the king undertook not to interfere directly within the lands of the lord of the soil. It closed the door to the king's officer, and the result was that in the long run the jurisdiction of the lord of the domain absorbed, at any rate to a large extent, the powers of the supreme state. It was quite otherwise with civic immunity. The privileged jurisdiction that it granted to the burghers, so far from weakening the jurisdiction of the state, strengthened it. Instead of escaping from the sovereign authority, the town, by the grant of a local court, attached itself directly to it. Its *échevins* were, if a modern form of expression may be permitted, a state magistracy. It was by no means the case that the prince's officer could not gain admittance; on the contrary it was he who presided over the court and executed its sentences. In short the town was in the full sense of the term a district under the law of the state. From this point of view, it stands in the sharpest contrast to the jurisdictions of the lords, and those, who have seen in it a corporate lordship, have been deceived by appearances.

Let us now glance at the composition of the municipal tribunal. In spite of differences in detail, we see in it a simple adaptation of the ordinary public law court of the Frankish period. Nowhere did the institution of the municipal magistracy (*échevinage*) strike root so deep as in Belgium.[1] It survived the political partitions of the 10th century. It is found, almost intact, in all the principalities that were subsequently set up between the sea and the Ardennes. The princes suffered it to remain in the magistracies of the various counties that they brought together under their power. In Flanders, for example, it is certain that, in most of the districts attached to castles, there were *échevins* in the *castrum* which reared itself as the local capital, who extended their jurisdiction over the whole of the district. At first, then, the immigrants into the *portus* were under the jurisdiction of this tribunal, because the tribunal itself regarded all free men as subject to the jurisdiction of the state. Then, when the moment came to give the towns their special magistrates, nothing was more natural than to gratify them by granting them an *échevinage* of their own. The region ruled by the town, broken off from the territorial district of which it had been part, received an organization based on the same lines as that of the older local court. Like the *échevins* of the

1. It is even quite possible that the *échevinage* was merely a local modification of the institution of the *rachimburgs,* a modification peculiar to the Meuse valley, where the greater part of the possessions of the Carolingians lay. There Charles the Great may have perfected it before extending it to the whole of *Francia.*

castle and its district, the *échevins* of the town were
the people's judges, chosen from among the inhabitants. Both alike were summoned and presided over
by the prince's officer, that is by the castellan. Even
the traditional number of twelve was preserved. Only,
instead of judging according to the old custom, the
échevins of the town judged according to the new law
of the burgher body; instead of meeting in the
borough (the castle), they met in the suburb of the
traders, either in the market hall or in the parish
churchyard. At the same time the territorial *échevins*
continued to meet near by in the *castrum* and to judge
the dependents of the castelry. It still remained *in*
the town, though no longer acting *for* the town. At
Bruges the *landhuis* of the *Franc*[1] still stands by the
side of the *gemeentehuis* (the town hall), reminding us
of the far distant day when the town was granted its
own *échevins,* analogous to, but independent of, the
older territorial magistrates.

From the 10th century the prince was the instrument and the guardian of the law of the state. Hence
the tribunal of the *échevins,* as a state tribunal, was
under the prince. Moreover, as we have just seen, its
president was a representative, or rather an officer,
of the prince, and it must be added that the prince
interfered in the nomination of its members. But the
échevins were at the same time a tribunal of the
commune, as might easily be inferred. Indeed, not
only was the court recruited from among the inhabitants of the town, but the law which it administered

1. The "liberty of Bruges" (*Franc* de Bruges) was in the later
Middle Ages the term applied to those parts of the original châtellenie
of Bruges which were outside the town and the region immediately
adjacent to it which had become subject, like the town, to the
municipal magistrates.

was solely the work of the burgher community. The law according to which it judged was, as the Fleming said, a *keure*, that is to say a law "chosen" by the burgesses, an exceptional law, which the prince recognized and ratified, but which did not emanate from him or from territorial custom. Hence the magistrates, charged with the execution of the town law, could not be a mere excrescence on the town population. It was necessary that they should be a part of it, that they should belong to it. And indeed, from the 11th century, the texts call the *échevins* indifferently *échevins* of the burghers and *échevins* of the prince. Thus their constitution was complex. They belonged at once to the feudal and to the communal organization, and, as time goes on, the second characteristic becomes more and more strongly marked. For the more it developed and increased in complexity, the more the law of the town formed part and parcel of the very life of the commune. All sorts of additions, rendered indispensable by the growing needs of municipal activity, were soon made to the original *keure*. Administrative regulations made their appearance; measures of every kind were enforced. The task of looking after the enforcement of these ordinances and of punishing the infraction of them naturally fell to the *échevins*. Thereafter they are not only the tribunal of the town, but also its *council*. At a period when the powers of the municipal court were not yet differentiated from one another, it united the attributes of judge and administrator. Without ceasing to belong to the prince, it belonged more and more to the commune. To it the guild, which had at first undertaken the relief of the most pressing needs of the trading population, henceforth surrendered its charge. The council collected the taxes, looked after public works such as the maintenance of the fortifications, the paving of the streets, etc., and exercised the guardianship of orphans. Side by side with its judicial functions, which it derived from the prince, it thus acquired administrative functions, delegated to it by the commune, and it won them by the force of circumstances and without being able to justify them by any legal title.

No doubt this absorption of the *échevins* by the town was sometimes attended with difficulties. The evolution which we have just described was only achieved in the lay principalities. The bishops, and the powerful ecclesiastical corporations that gathered round them in the cities,[1] strove, on the contrary, to impede it. At Liége, Cambrai, and Utrecht, the bishop struggled with varying success to keep the *échevins* under his power exclusively. We have already seen the motives for that conduct, and we need not recur to them. Its result was to compel the burghers to institute, on their own account, a council charged to maintain their interests, by the side of the prince's tribunal, and often in opposition to it. This council, whose members usually took the name of " sworn men " (*jurés, jurati*), held its power from the burgesses of the town. It was their nominee, the executor of their wishes; upon them alone it depended,

1. All through the Middle Ages the name of city was reserved for towns which had a bishop, whatever their importance otherwise. Thérouanne, which was never anything but a large market town, was a city; on the other hand Ghent, the most powerful town in the whole of Belgium, was not a city. In the following pages I shall conform to the ancient usage.

as the *échevins* depended upon the prince. It was created to prevent the interference of the prince in municipal affairs. To a certain extent it may be regarded as an instrument of revolution, and in this connexion it is interesting to observe that it was established by a *conjuration,* that is by an alliance of all the inhabitants, sealed by an oath. The power of the commune is thus more clearly seen in the episcopal cities than in the towns subject to lay lords. There, owing to the attitude of the bishops, it is in no way amalgamated with the state authority.[1]

It must not be supposed that in the Low Countries the commune was a phenomenon peculiar to certain towns. The actual truth is that in this country we do not encounter communes with political aims, organised on the French model, where all powers flow from the association of townsmen. The " cities " did approach this form of organization but they never attained it fully. Elsewhere it is not to be met with.[2] Instead what we do find everywhere, is the commune in so far as it was a corporate unity, including all the burghers, and so far as it was in the eyes of the law a collective personality. In the towns where there were *jurati,* as well as in those where there were none, the inhabitants constituted a society, a corporation, whose

1. M. Vanderkindere has tried to show that the opposition between the princely power and the power of the commune was a primitive and universal fact. See his study entitled " La première phase de l'évolution politique des villes flamandes," *Annales du Nord et de l'Est,* 1905. He endeavours to discover the *jurés* in opposition to the *échevins* in all the Flemish towns. But the texts which he cites, and which I naturally cannot examine here, are not in my opinion decisive. See the short remarks which I have made on this point in my *Histoire de Belgique,* vol. i (3rd edition), p. 198.

2. At least only exceptionally in the 13th century when the counts of Flanders introduced it into certain localities, as, for example, at Deynze.

E

members were answerable for one another. No one was a burgher unless he had taken the oath to the commune, which bound him closely to all the other burghers. The burgher's person and goods belonged to the town, and they, no less than he, could at any moment be requisitioned for its service. An isolated burgher is as unthinkable as an isolated man in primitive times. In barbarous times a man was only a person by virtue of the family community to which he belonged; in mediæval times he was a burgher by virtue of the civic community of which he was a part. Nothing perhaps, among all the social organisms created by man, recalls more strongly the societies of the animal kingdom—I refer here to ants and bees— than do the mediæval communes. In both cases there is the same subordination of the individual to the whole, the same co-operation for the sake of a livelihood, for the maintenance and defence of the community, the same hostility towards the stranger, the same pitiless disregard of the useless.

Perpetual banishment was the most characteristic punishment of town law. From the 12th century the *homo inutilis ville,* to use the characteristic expression of contemporary documents, was driven out remorselessly. If, in the town, property was not subject to the inroads of the overlord's power, if it had no longer to satisfy all the feudal rights, which in the country at large still weighed upon its inheritance, mortmain, heriot, *buteil, corimede,* etc., nevertheless it did not escape the taxation of the community. Not only did the municipality in case of need dip into its members' pockets by means of direct taxes and forced loans, but the goods of each burgher severally were chargeable with the town's debts, and he could not take his goods with him, if he left the town, without paying for a permit to depart (*droit d'issue*).

In one point, and that an essential one, the commune differs from the hive or the ant hill. So far as we can compare the insect communities with any exactitude to human societies, they are governed on monarchical principles. The commune on the contrary, at any rate during its earliest times and, in theory, even later, was democratic. At the very period when the principle of monarchy was dominant in every feudal state, the commune expressed the ideal of the government of the people by the people. The power that the magistrates exercised was delegated to them by it. They acted in the name of the *communitas* or *universitas civium*. If the town recognized the sovereignty of the territorial prince, if it paid him taxes and served under him in time of war, it was nevertheless independent in the sphere of the town's own interests. The corporation of burghers was self-governing. All its members enjoyed the same rights and submitted to the same obligations. The country outside was patriarchal in its organization.[1] In the town the idea of paternal power was replaced by that of brotherhood. The members of the guilds and the *carités* already treated one another as brothers, and from these select associations the word passed to the association as a whole. *Unus subveniat alteri tanquam fratri suo* said the *keure* of Aire; " let each man help his fellow as his brother."

No doubt the social differences between the brethren within the commune were numerous and striking ; at

1. Compare the word senior = elder.

a very early date a minority of wealthy men arose among the inhabitants. But there was not at first any political privilege corresponding to the superiority in fortune. In Flanders, at the beginning of the 13th century, the only qualification required for an *échevin* was a good name, irrespective of his wealth. But it is evident that, as a matter of fact, from the very beginning municipal power was exercised by the most opulent. That is a state of affairs inherent in all democracies, so far as their conflicts are independent of economic strife. Now during their first period, that is to say until well into the 13th century, this strife, although existing in embryo in the social constitution of the burghers, had not yet broken out. At that period the great object of the towns was to provide themselves with institutions that made life possible, and at that essential task all without distinction, " the great " and " the less," rich and poor, worked with one accord. Contrary to what happened in ancient times, the history of the town populations of the Middle Ages begins with democratic government. Social equality did not exist among its members, but all with the same title and the same rights belonged to the commune, and shared in its government.

CHAPTER III.

THE GROWTH OF URBAN INSTITUTIONS.
(*Continued.*)

I. Original and Derived Types of Town Constitution.—II. The Liége Type.—III. The Flemish Type.

I.

Original and Derived Types of Town Constitution.

In the preceding pages we have tried to describe the general features of town growth. Most of them are not confined exclusively to the Low Countries. We find them, with local modifications, more or less marked, all over Western Europe. Still it is perhaps in the basins of the Meuse and the Scheldt that they are most clearly defined. We have already seen that, with very few exceptions, all the towns of that region are the offspring of the Middle Ages, and that neither their situation nor their plan was influenced by survivals of the Roman Empire. Above all, it should be added that commercial and industrial activity, the chief source of Belgian town life, developed with special vigour along the two rivers on whose banks the towns were situated. Having tried to describe the permanent common factors of this development, we must glance at the different local forms in which they were realised.

These varieties are very numerous, and in the Low Countries as elsewhere, towns fall into easily distin-

guishable "families." The towns of Flanders, of
Liége, of Brabant, and of Holland constitute so many
groups, or types, as they may fairly be called, of
municipal constitution.

In each of the great territorial principalities, the
institutions of the communes betray a close relation-
ship. Nowhere in the Low Countries do we find the
phenomenon, so common in France, of a number of
places belonging to different districts and depending
on different lords, adopting the law peculiar to some
town whose charter they take as a model. Nothing
recalls for example the wide diffusion of the " establishments " of Rouen or of Saint-Quentin.[1] Everywhere the town's law was evolved on the spot. It was
adapted to the special circumstances governing it, and
borrowed nothing from outside.

It is furthermore instructive to observe that this law
is in no way the work of lawgivers, analogous to the
nomothetae of antiquity. Although in many towns
local tradition preserves the name of a founder, we
should seek in vain in their institutions for any
suggestion of their being due to his personal initiative.
No doubt the municipal charters are promulgated in
the prince's name, but it is a very easy task to show
that they are confined to ratifying a situation already
existing *de facto*, or to granting institutions demanded
by the inhabitants. In the Low Countries municipal

1. See the works of A. Giry, *Les établissements de Rouen* (1883)
and *Les établissements de Saint-Quentin* (1887). Naturally I am
here only speaking of the early period of the spontaneous growth of
municipal institutions; later, from the end of the 12th century,
towns were artificially created complete in all respects, and the law
slowly elaborated in the old towns was transferred to them. In the
13th century the counts of Holland systematically extended the law of
the towns of Holland to the towns of Friesland when they conquered
it.

constitutions are the direct outcome of the free play of
civic life. They are the product of economic and
social circumstances. Like feudal institutions, they
answered to the demands of a particular moment in
the development of those circumstances; to these they
adapted themselves, and in town and fief alike it is
impossible to discern, at the beginning, either the
working of any particular national characteristic or the
action of a legislator.

It is only in localities where commerce developed
early, and with sufficient intensity to attract settlers in
great numbers, that municipal institutions were created.
It is quite true that, from the end of the 13th century,
towns were scattered over the whole surface of the
Low Countries. But a close inspection shows that
most of them were only towns with institutions derived
from the few primitive and original types. The municipal movement, spreading from certain centres,
gained ground bit by bit in proportion as commercial
activity extended, and permeated more deeply the
social organism. The privileged status of the burgher
spread with it. From the banks of the rivers, where
it first appeared, it ascended their tributaries and
reached first the plains and then the upper valleys.
Small boroughs, small market towns, even simple
villages were transformed, and exacted or received
from their lords municipal institutions. But it is
not by studying such cases that we shall grasp the
proper nature of these constitutions. We must begin
with the primitive and original type rather than with
the derived types. Because this fact has been too
often overlooked, a question, which is after all a
simple one, has become unduly complicated. The

survivals of the seignorial rule of the country districts, which have been preserved in towns of late growth, have been wrongly regarded as the origins of all municipal organization. An attempt has thus been made to connect the beginnings of town constitutions either with the ancient judicial organization of the Frankish period, or with the Germanic " mark," [1] or with the village community. It is quite evident that a sound method ought to follow a different course. We ought to go back to the fountain head, and study the growth of the burgher communities at the point where they first arise. We must not look for the secret of the origin of civic life in towns of the second order. It is rather to be found in the primitive centres of commerce, that is to say, in those localities specially favoured by nature which became great mercantile cities. Everywhere else we shall find only late imitations, more or less successful, copies more or less exact.

Of the divers types of civic organization in the Low Countries only two are sufficiently well known to be described in this book; the Liége type and the Flemish type. The institutions of the town in the northern Netherlands are not known to us until the 13th century with the exception of Utrecht, which, however, presents a great resemblance to Liége. Although we possess earlier information about the towns of Brabant, we are by no means in a position to describe them as precisely as we can their neighbours on the East and West. But Flanders and the

1. I allude here to G. L. von Maurer's formerly widely accepted theory. L. Vanderkindere has tried to apply it to the Low Countries in his interesting study entitled *Notice sur l'origine des magistrats communaux et sur l'organisation de la marke dans nos contrées.* Brussels (1874).

bishopric of Liége present two particularly characteristic types, to which the towns of the other territories more or less closely conform.

We will begin with the bishopric of Liége, whose municipal institutions, less highly developed than those of Flanders, will enable us, by the contrast they offer, to understand better the originality of the latter.

II.

THE LIÉGE TYPE.

The bishopric of Liége was one of the numerous episcopal states set up by the emperors in the course of the 10th and 11th centuries. Formed by successive donations of counties and domains, it was never such a coherent whole as the lay principalities, which were due to the continuous encroachments of powerful dynasties extending from a central point. Yet strangely cut up as the bishop's lands were, it had in the Meuse from Givet to Maeseyck a geographical axis. Ever since the Carolingian period Maestricht (*Trajectum ad Mosam*), placed at the point where the old Roman road from Cologne to Boulogne crossed the river, had displayed a certain amount of commercial activity. Higher up, on the upper reaches of the Meuse, Huy and Dinant early devoted themselves to metal working. Between these towns and Maestricht, Liége itself, whither St. Hubert had transferred his see from Tongres about 710, was for a long time only an insignificant town. Its Carolingian prelates, however, occupied themselves with its embellishment; and, after the tempest of the Norman invasions, their successors, thanks to the steady favour of the emperors, energetically resumed the work which they had begun. From Stephen to Otbert (901—1119) the town saw seven collegiate churches and two great monasteries rise in succession around the cathedral and the bishop's palace. It girt itself with walls, and a stone bridge was thrown over the Meuse. At the same time the fame of its schools, drew to this "Athens of the North," eager bands of masters and scholars from all parts of Western Europe. About the year 1000 it was undoubtedly the first of the " cities " of the Low Countries. It was also distinguished by its essentially clerical character. Its trading population was inferior to that of Cambrai or Utrecht. The commerce of the principality had its chief seat at Maestricht; manufactures flourished at Huy and Dinant, but Liége was essentially a town of priests. Split up by monastic and other franchises, its soil belonged for the most part to chapters and abbeys. Its laymen consisted mainly of knights and *ministeriales,* who were at once the bishop's guard and his administrative agents. There were also the artisans who found their livelihood in administering to the needs of the clergy.

Under these conditions, it is not astonishing that the bishops succeeded without difficulty in setting up a very strong government. From the time of Notger (972—1008), we see them occupied in organizing their revenues, in taking measures for the defence of their lands, and in destroying the castles of the robber lords. In 1077 Henry of Verdun borrowed from France the institution of the Peace of God, and set up at Liége the *judicium pacis,* whose sphere of action included the whole diocese. We know enough about them to assert that the prelates spared no effort to improve and secure their subjects' position.

In their double capacity as ecclesiastics and great landed proprietors, the bishops did not get beyond an entirely patriarchal and authoritative conception of government. Excellent as it was for the rural population, their government weighed heavily on the burgher communities when urban life began to appear in the towns of the Meuse. The bishops were reluctant to allow them the autonomy they demanded, and in the long run there was sure to be a clashing of interests between a prince and the communes, because of their lack of mutual understanding or sympathy.

The first instance of a claim for town rights in the bishopric of Liége goes back to 1066. On the demand of the burghers of Huy, the bishop Theoduin granted them thenceforth the exclusive right of garrisoning the castle in the town, and the privilege of not answering his summons to the host in time of war until a fortnight after the men of Liége. The charter which was drawn up on that occasion also ratified a certain number of improvements in the customary law, which, however, the chronicler, Giles of Orval, has thought it good to pass over in silence, " for fear of wearying his readers." Still, from what he does tell us, we are led to regard the Huy document as one of the most ancient ratifications of what we have already called the burghers' political programme. Elsewhere Orval sketches clearly the behaviour of the bishops when confronted with this programme. Theoduin's concessions were not, in fact, spontaneous. The population had to purchase them by a money payment. They bought them for a third of their movable property, and nothing illustrates better the extent to which the accumulation of movable property by the traders effectively assisted social progress.

Is the preservation of Theoduin's charter to be attributed to a mere chance, or is it better explained by the precocious development of the trade of Huy? At any rate everything seems to show that the privileged position of Huy was earlier than that of the capital of the bishopric, which was so much less active from the economic point of view. But the movement that had begun was to be interrupted no longer. From the beginning of the 12th century it became necessary on all hands to yield to the demands of the burghers. Thenceforth the problem of the towns faced the bishops, and imperatively demanded a solution.

The solution discovered was a sort of compromise between the prerogatives of the prince and the tendency of the communes to complete autonomy. The Liége towns received all the privileges essential to their development. Each constituted a special judicial territory, possessing a court of justice of its own distinct from those of the country side. But this tribunal remained definitely the bishop's tribunal. Its *échevins,* the burghers' privileged judges, numbering twelve in the capital and seven in the other " good towns," were invariably named for life by the bishop and were partly drawn, at least until the end of the 12th century, from the *ministeriales.* They no doubt administered the law of the town, and were the guardians of town customs, but they in no wise present the aspect of a communal magistracy.

Henceforth the burghers of Huy devoted their best

energies to setting up, side by side with this semi-feudal law court, machinery for the government of their town which was entirely under their own control. They could afford to leave the judicial power in the hands of the *échevins,* but not to abandon to them the administration of public business. From the middle of the 12th century they provided themselves with sworn councillors, or *jurés,* who were elected by the townsfolk, took the oath in their presence and were charged with the care of the communal interests. The bishops, however, protested energetically against this illegal or, shall we say, extra-legal innovation. In 1230 one of them, John of Eppes, obtained from the emperor a decree formally forbidding " conjurations " and " communes " in all the kingdom of Germany. But the towns found the need of an independent magistracy too pressing. The *jurés,* whose establishment was in the first instance due to an insurrection, became permanent in course of time. After the revolt of all the towns of the bishopric, in the time of Henry of Gelderland (1247—1274), a rising connected with the name of Henry of Dinant, their position as an integral part of the local municipal constitutions was definitely secured. Henceforth the *jurés* and two " masters " formed the Council. But this council did not succeed in absorbing the jurisdiction of the *échevins.* Jurisdiction over landed property, criminal cases and other important matters remained in their hands until the end of the Middle Ages.[1] More than that, it was not till the 14th century

1. In technical language " la haute justice " remained to the échevins, while " la basse justice " was in the hands of the municipal authority. For the distinction between " high " and " low " justice see Beaumanoir, *Coutumes de Beauvaisis,* ch. lviii.

that they disappeared from the council and ceased to interfere in the administration of the city.   The *perron*,[1] which had at first been the symbol of the episcopal jurisdiction, was at the same period to become, by a significant development, the emblem of the communal autonomy.

Thus, in the bishopric of Liége, municipal institutions presented two distinct groups of magistrates differing in character and period of origin.   The more ancient, the *échevins*, formed a tribunal belonging to the lord ; the later, the *jurés*, the sworn members of the council, were the nominees and the representatives of the commune.   The first administered justice in the name of the bishop, the second in the name of the burghers.   The competence of the *jurés* extended only to municipal regulations and police jurisdiction.   The law terms in use at Liége exactly expressed that competence by the phrase " statutable jurisdiction," while that of the *échevins* was called " legal jurisdiction." This distinction persisted to the end.   In spite of attempts, to which we shall have to refer later, the towns of the bishopric never succeeded in bringing the episcopal tribunal under their own control.

III.

THE FLEMISH TYPE.

Very different is the spectacle presented by the towns of the county of Flanders.   Here, municipal institutions were established without collisions or

1. The *perron* at Liége, which has been much discussed, was in its origin simply a cross marking the episcopal immunity in the city. On the institutions of Liége, see G. Kurth's recent book, *La cité de Liége au Moyen Age*. Brussels, 1910.

conflicts with the prince, and were developed much
more completely. That is not attributable to a
difference of race. It would be a serious mistake
to think that the Flanders of the Middle Ages was, as
contrasted with the Walloon district on the banks of
the Meuse, a purely Germanic country. As a matter
of fact from the reign of Arnulf I. (918—965), the
county of Flanders was for a long time bilingual.
Extending from the Scheldt to the Canche, it included,
exactly like the modern Belgium, a Flemish speaking
population in the north, and a population of Latin
speech in the south. It was not till after the conquests
first of Philip Augustus, who took away Artois from
Flanders, and then of Philip the Fair, who took
possession of the lordships of Lille, Douai and Orchies,
that its population became exclusively low-Dutch in
race. But before that time the burghers of Arras, like
the burghers of Bruges or Ghent, were regarded as
Flemings and lived under the same institutions.
Municipal constitutions showed the same characteristics to the north of the linguistic frontier as to the
south, and no better example could be quoted to show
how true it was that the growth of the towns was in
all essentials due to their environment, and was
independent of peculiarities of race.

The environment was in this case exceptionally
favourable. Even more than the Meuse, the Scheldt
was a great commercial artery, and the district
possessed also the immeasurable advantage of being
washed by the sea along the whole of its western
frontier. The coast, indented by the estuaries of the
Canche, the Yser and the Zwyn, furnished excellent
natural harbours, while the Rhine and the Meuse

mingled their waters with those of the Scheldt, and thus gave access to Flemish soil, to the boatmen who navigated those streams.[1] Flanders, destined by nature to become a rendezvous for merchants, was quick to profit by such an advantageous position. At Messines, Thourout, Ypres, Lille and Douai great fairs were held under the special protection of the counts and there, from the beginning of the 12th century at latest, Italians came into contact with the traders of the North. The Norman conquest of England, by bringing that country, which had hitherto lived in comparative isolation, into constant relations with the continent, further increased the economic activity of the Flemish region. Between the estuaries of the Zwyn and the Thames, which faced one another, intercourse was henceforth uninterrupted, and grew steadily year by year. From this time the great island had for the commerce of the county an importance that was to increase until the end of the Middle Ages. And this is easily intelligible, when we remember that the wool for the Flemish cloth was supplied by England. For Flanders was not only a commercial district. It was just as much, and perhaps even more, an industrial district and it is to this fact that it owes its especial peculiarities.

From the earliest times the population of the coast had manufactured woollen fabrics. The large flocks of sheep, fed on the sea-side pastures behind the dunes, furnished the raw material in abundance. In Roman times the fabrics of the *Morini* and the *Menapii* had enjoyed a certain repute. The invasion of the Franks

1. For the specially favourable geographical conditions of the district see R. Blanchard, *La Flandre*, 1906.

did not put an end to their manufacture. The new inhabitants learnt their craft from the vanquished. In the 9th century the cloaks known as Frisian, which were spread abroad over the Rhineland, and were noteworthy for their fine colours and excellent weaving, came originally from the district of Thérouanne. Thus good fortune willed that the Flemish cloth manufacturers should begin by developing under the industrial tradition.of Rome, and consequently should profit by a privileged position.

Though clothmaking was at first practised by the peasants of the coast, it could not fail to make its home in the towns as soon as they came into existence. It would be immensely interesting to know how this transference from country to town was accomplished. From lack of documents we are obliged to put the question aside. But we can easily understand that the country weavers must have migrated in a body to those places where they found, besides buyers for their produce, the protection of ramparts and personal liberty. In the 12th century all the Flemish towns became largely employed in the cloth trade. We find their traders chiefly engaged in exporting stuffs. Production far surpassed local needs and found ever widening outlets abroad. Soon the native wool no longer sufficed to supply the industry; it became necessary to procure raw material from outside, and the weavers obtained it from England, where the moist pastures nourished a breed of sheep with thick and silky fleeces. From the 12th century till the end of the Middle Ages, Flanders was the island kingdom's best customer. The merchants of the towns used to cross the sea to sell their cloth, and

F

brought back full cargoes of wool. To appreciate the importance of this trade, it is sufficient to recall here the formation of the Hansa of London, a powerful association of local guilds devoted to trade with England.

No excuse is necessary for dwelling at length on the economic activity of Flanders. Nowhere in fact were the towns so entirely the offspring of commerce. Nothing smothered its vigorous impulse and no resistance availed against it. Neither the church nor the nobles succeeded in stopping the advance of the burgher communities, which are here seen in their purest and, if the expression may be used, their most classic form. The count of Flanders alone could have hindered their progress seriously. But statesmanship was no more dependent on the individual will in the Middle Ages than in our own times. It has always had to bow to local circumstances. If the behaviour of the bishops to their towns is explained, not by the caprice of the prelates, but by the impossibility of ceding the administration of the "cities," which were the centres of their diocesan activities, to the communes, that of the counts of Flanders shows clearly, in spite of certain unimportant episodes, that they understood what profit was to be gained from the remarkable vigour of commerce in their territory. Their interest led them to favour its development, and they did not fail to do so. They promulgated laws expressly enjoining respect for the traders and for all men from other lands, traversing their country. Charles the Good (1119—1127) is praised by a contemporary for having imposed on Flanders the discipline and quiet of a monastery, and the day that the news of his assassination reached Ypres, the traders, who had assembled for the fair, hastened to disperse. Similarly, the counts provided for the needs of the *portus,* those permanent stations of the trade which enriched them. They were watchful guardians of the growing towns, and did all they could to help them to establish the new system of law which was indispensable to them.

From the reign of Robert the Frisian (1071—1093), it may be assumed that the cause of the prince and the cause of the towns were bound up together. In fact when Robert forcibly wrested the county from his nephew Arnulf, he was energetically backed up by all the burgher communities of the coast, and we may be sure that they reaped a handsome reward. A little later, in 1127 and 1128, they rose to avenge the death of the good count Charles, the victim of a plot hatched by a party among the nobles. They refused to acknowledge William of Normandy, except at the price of exorbitant concessions, rejected him when they saw him abandon them for the support of the feudal element, and set Thierry of Alsace on the throne. The house of Alsace never forgot to whom it owed its power.

It is not astonishing that the counts early employed their influence in favour of the towns and gave legal sanction to their claims. Little by little the counts granted the various demands of their programme of reform. Trial by combat was abolished; restrictions were imposed upon ecclesiastical jurisdiction; military service was limited to cases of resisting invasion. All these concessions went hand in hand with the grant of commercial privileges. The count renounced *seewerp*[1] and gave up his right to market dues in favour of the guilds.

The crisis of 1127 gave an opportunity for completing all these concessions and, so to speak, crystallizing them, in the charters of the towns. William of Normandy agreed to everything so as to win the support of the towns. They dictated their terms to him, and, though we have lost the charter granted to Bruges, we still possess in that of Saint-Omer the proof that, by that date, the development of the town was achieved in Flanders.[2]

A striking characteristic of the municipal law of this district is its uniformity. At first, no doubt, there must have been local differences. But in the reign of Philip of Alsace (1168—1191) all the great towns obtained the same institutions and were governed by identical *keures*, so that the rights and duties of each measured the extent and guaranteed the security of all. All too, being treated with the same consideration, occupied the same position in relation to the prince, and receiving equal protection from him showed the same respect for his authority.[3]

Curiously enough it was the charter of the French-speaking town of Arras which became the basis of the rights of the Flemish towns, by extension to the

1. Right of flotsam and jetsam.
2. Flanders possesses no charter older than that of Saint-Omer. The attempt to assign the charter of Grammont to 1068 has failed. In reality the document belongs to the end of the 12th century. See V. Fris, *Bull. de la Soc. d'Histoire et d'Archéologie de Gand*, 1905, p. 219.
3. L. Vanderkindere, in his study of " La Politique de Philippe d'Alsace et ses conséquences," *Bull. de l'Acad. de Belgique, Classe des Lettres*, 1905, p. 749, thinks, on the contrary, that Philip was hostile to the communes. I have elsewhere (*Histoire de Belgique*, vol. i, 3rd ed., p. 198) given my reasons for not accepting his view.

other towns of the county, though most of them were
in the Flemish-speaking district. The type of organization that it shews is very simple. Each town was
withdrawn from the territorial *échevinage* (jurisdiction) of the lordship in which it lay, but had its own
échevins, generally twelve or thirteen in number.
Chosen by the count, but selected exclusively from the
burghers, the new *échevins* were able to act in a double
capacity. They were the prince's judges, and he
deputed one of his own officers to preside over them,
first the castellan and, later, beginning in the 12th
century, his bailiff; but these judges were, at the same
time, the councillors of the commune. They thus
indicated in a significant manner the good understanding that existed between the sovereign power
and the aspirations of the municipalities. The dupli-
cation of the magistracies, which we have seen in
the Liége district, where each of the opposing parties
was clearly distinguished from its rival, did not
exist here. The great Flemish towns, that is to
say those powerful commercial centres in which
municipal law was developed, knew nothing of
the *jurés.* They are only met with in places of
secondary importance, the small towns belonging to
a local lord, from whom it was necessary to wrest
concessions. In 1127, when the towns demanded of
William of Normandy an organization of their own
choice, they spoke only of *échevins.* The count's
authority over the *échevins* was, moreover, very
slight. Though he nominated them, there is no
evidence that he could depose them, and in fact it
seems likely that in practice he confined himself to
ratifying their choice as each vacancy occurred. On

the other hand though the count's officer sat in their court, he was forbidden to take part in its deliberations when the affairs of the commune were under discussion. Thus municipal autonomy developed freely in Flanders under the prince's protection. In the first half of the 13th century, it is still more clearly confirmed by the transformation of the *échevinage* from a magistracy for life, as it was to begin with, into an annual office. This innovation was introduced upon the demand of the burghers. First mentioned at Arras in 1194, it gradually spread over the north of the county. Ypres obtained the privilege in 1209, Ghent in 1212, Douai in 1228, Lille in 1235, Bruges in 1241. It is not difficult to divine the motives of the change. There was, no doubt, a desire not to leave the government of the town in the hands of men too old to bear the heavy burden of an *échevin's* functions, but there was also a desire to strengthen the municipal character of the civic magistracy. Indeed the annual *échevins* were no longer exclusively nominated by the count. The charters formally recognized the right to present the burghers of the preceding year, or to set up a more or less complicated system of election, under which the town collaborated with the prince in the appointment of its judge-administrators. Further rules were set up which distributed the seats of the *échevins* among the different parishes of the commune, and this innovation emphasized once more the capture of the *échevinage* by the burghers. The count's rights did not disappear, but they were then, and remained until the end of the 14th century, nominal rather than effective.

Up to the end the count had still an official representative in the commune, who provided him with a very real excuse for interfering in its affairs. However extensive was the autonomy of the commune, it did not altogether destroy the prince's power within its walls. It did not even attempt to do so. Until the end of the 12th century the castellan, in his quality of "viscount," represented the territorial lord in the midst of the commune. Indeed these castellans, holding their office by hereditary right, like all the functionaries during the agricultural period of the Middle Ages, regarded their charge as a fief and used it for their own profit. Collisions between these feudal officers and the burghers were inevitable. The count seized his opportunity. His interest urged him to destroy the influence of the castellans and to substitute his authority for theirs. He consequently upheld the burghers against them, therein imitating the conduct of the French kings, who at the same period espoused the cause of the communes against their lords. In the reign of Philip of Alsace, the castellans everywhere gave way before the coalition of the burghers and the prince. They disappeared, or retained only some trifling revenues or some honorary distinctions. In their place there now appeared a new kind of official, a bailiff.

The bailiff was a paid servant, removable at pleasure, and had nothing feudal about him. His office was clearly another result of the same economic change that had made town life possible. Like the towns themselves, the bailiff could not have come into existence but for the great growth of commercial prosperity in the Flemish towns. This movement created movable property alongside landed property,

and developed the supply and circulation of money.
It substituted for the old offices, which were trans-
mitted from father to son with the estates to which
they were attached, institutions directly dependent on
public authority. These were entrusted to agents
appointed by such authority, and living on the salary
which it was now in a position to pay them. Thus
it is not at all surprising that, as the economic
development began earlier in Flanders than in the
neighbouring countries, the bailiffs, like the towns
themselves, appeared there sooner than anywhere else.

Between the bailiff and the *échevins* the contrast was
striking. The latter were the representatives of the
commune, the former was the instrument of the count.
It was only to the prince that the bailiff tendered his
accounts; it was only to the prince that he owed
obedience. Continually replaced, and always chosen
from outside the burghers of the town in which his
administrative duty lay, the bailiff was responsible
only to the sovereign lord who nominated and paid
him.

Sooner or later such a situation was sure to lead to
conflicts between the magistrates of the commune and
the officials of the prince, since the two authorities
were not so much co-ordinate as merely contiguous.
The first represented the autonomy of the town, the
second the territorial authority, and little by little the
contrast between them became more striking and more
dangerous. This contrast makes itself seen from the
middle of the 13th century. The beautiful harmony,
which had so long prevailed as regards the relations
of the count and the towns, gave place to a fierce
rivalry. The ideal of the great communes became

republican, at the same time that the prince aimed at monarchy. The prince tried to increase his sovereignty while the town strove to extend its privileges. The end of the Middle Ages will shew us the two rival powers engaged in a desperate struggle. The causes and vicissitudes of this strife we shall in due course have to examine.

CHAPTER IV.

THE ECONOMICS OF THE TOWN.

I. Economic Relations between Town and Country.—II. Regulation of the Town Food Supply and the Trade in Foodstuffs.—III. Regulation of the Lesser Industries. The Crafts.—IV. Regulation of the Exporting Industries. Wage Earners and Capitalists. V. The Economic Aspect of the Episcopal Cities.—VI. Density of the Town Population.

I.

Economic Relations between Town and Country.

The reader, who has followed us so far, will have seen that the origin of mediæval towns was essentially due to an economic transformation. The city of the Middle Ages presents to the eye of the historian a much simpler form than the ancient city. In the case of the latter, the first glance reveals to us the working of the national and religious factors as well as the economic. On the other hand the organization both of the church and of the state in the Middle Ages are of much earlier origin than the municipal institutions; consequently the church and the state are both perfectly distinct from the municipality. Though many towns were the seat of a bishopric or of some representative of the central state, such conditions were not essential to civic development. In the Low Countries particularly, most of the important communities, such as Ghent, Bruges, Brussels, Valenciennes, etc., were only markets and industrial centres.   Economic activity, economic needs, left their mark upon the whole of the social constitution and gave it a peculiar character.   Before tracing the history of this constitution, and undertaking an examination of the special forms which it assumed under democratic government, it is necessary to describe briefly the chief features of municipal economics.   This is all the more important because the generally accepted ideas on this subject are not applicable without important qualifications to the towns of Belgium.   We shall find ourselves obliged, then, to modify appreciably a theory which, starting from an imperfect analysis of civic life, quite fails to explain its characteristics in the parts of Europe where it was most strongly developed.   This disadvantage would doubtless have been avoided if, instead of illustrating municipal economics by examples of late date and incomplete development, historians had bestowed their chief attention upon the earliest and most powerful communities.   What we have already had occasion to say about institutions is justified afresh in this connexion.   The original centres of civic development ought obviously to be chosen as the starting point for scientific enquiry.   In this respect Flanders claims a pre-eminent place in the study of these difficult questions.   Perhaps the pages which follow will prove the accuracy of this statement.

The most striking economic feature of the town is its sterility.   In other words, the town, left to itself, could not support its inhabitants.   It might possess quite an extensive dependent territory, and, like many towns of our own time, numerous cow-houses and pig-styes. Yet it still remains true that, without the continual importation of food-stuffs from the country-side, its population would have been doomed to die of hunger. The village and the great domain were self-supporting; not so the town, which could not subsist without them. Like the clerk and the noble, the burgher was incapable of providing *directly* for his daily wants. But his position was much more unfavourable than that of the noble or the clerk. They were the actual owners of the soil. If they did not work themselves, they received its produce, since it belonged to them, and their subsistence was permanently assured by the labour of their vassals. The burghers, on the other hand, did not own either serfs or estates. They had no claim to the produce of the soil. To get possession of such produce, they had to buy it, or, perhaps we should say, to exchange for it the commodities which they manufactured. Instead of being economically independent, their lives were perpetually dependent on the help of the peasants and the landed proprietors of the neighbourhood. That help, without which their continued existence was impossible, they could not legally demand.

The country folk, on the other hand, of their own accord and by the mere force of economic circumstances, brought their commodities to the neighbouring town for sale. It gave them what they had lacked till its appearance; a market for their corn and their cattle. From the day of its foundation, the peasants ceased to be at once the self-sufficing producers and the consumers of the fruits of the earth. The old rural domestic economy, by which each man only cultivated and gathered what he required for his own support, disappeared from the moment that the colonies of traders and artisans became anxious to obtain the fruits of the husbandman's labour. Henceforth the peasant also became buyer and seller. He sold to the burgher the produce of the soil and, in return, bought from him the utensils and the clothing that he had formerly been obliged to make for himself, according to the primitive methods of rustic craft. At the same time and as a direct consequence, he sowed and culti- vated more land, sure always of finding a buyer for the crops which he raised from the soil. His plough broke up the waste; his axe felled the trees of the neighbouring forest, and the smoke from his " clearings " went up from the moorland. It was as though the infection of a new activity had spread from the infant towns to the open country, and roused the peasant from his age-long torpor. His lot improved rapidly. Serfdom declined, and in districts like Flanders, where towns were particularly numerous, it disappeared almost completely in the course of the 13th century. The lords themselves hastened its suppression. For the awakening of the country, under the influence of civic life, prevented them from maintaining intact the system of managing their estates that had had its day. The fall in the value of money was an inevitable consequence of the increased stock of coin, and the importance of this factor kept pace with the growing activity of trade; but it also steadily lessened the value of the fixed and hereditary pay- ments received from their vassals. The increased profits from the soil all went to the peasants. There was only one means by which the great proprietors could in their turn reap any benefit from them : they freed their serfs, and leased to them the lands which they had so long possessed by hereditary right, but at the expense of their liberty.

II.

THE REGULATION OF THE TOWN FOOD SUPPLY AND OF THE TRADE IN FOODSTUFFS.

Thus the town necessarily brought the burgher and the peasant into economic relations. The surrounding country sustained the town in its midst. One of the first duties of the municipal government was to see that the intercourse between the two was as full and easy as possible. Hence very soon—in Flanders from the second half of the 12th century—there followed a whole series of public works : improvement of roads, repairing of waterways, and the establishment of weekly markets (Friday Markets, etc.). But the most important consequence was a very special legislation with a view to the town's supply of food.

That legislation, of which some remains still survive to our own days in the police regulation of the municipal markets, was inspired exclusively by the interests of the burghers. Its object was to secure for the townsman a plentiful supply of necessaries at a low price. It was quickly recognized that each set of middle-men, through whose hands commodities passed on their way from the producer to the consumer, inevitably raised the price. Hence it was needful to bring the countryman, who wished to sell, face to face with the townsman who wished to buy, and to prevent a group of speculators from making a corner in provisions. We have only to look over the communal regulations from this point of view, to realize that this is the spirit that animated them. The *lettre des vénaux* of Liége in 1317 forbade "engrossers" buying, within a radius of two leagues round the city, poultry, cheese or venison. All these commodities had to be brought to the market, and it was only when the burghers were sufficiently provided for, that traders were allowed to acquire wholesale the unsold surplus. Butchers were prohibited from keeping meat in their cellars; bakers might not procure more corn than they required for their own baking. The most minute precautions were taken to prevent any artificial raising of prices. Not only was a *maximum* established, but also selling outside the market was strictly forbidden. In other words it was an offence to sell goods otherwise than in public, under the eye of the burghers and the officers of the commune. To such lengths was the idea carried that at Saint-Trond, the burgher who kept pigeons for his own amusement, was not allowed to sell them to his neighbours. If he wanted to get rid of them, he might only eat them himself or offer them for sale in the market.

It is useless to insist further on these stipulations, the number of which could be increased indefinitely. Strange as they appear, they are easily explicable if we refer them to the principle of which they were the applications.

This principle was that of compulsory direct ex-

change[1] instituted for the benefit of the buyer. Of
the two parties face to face in the market, the producer
from the country and the town buyer, the latter only
was considered. The prohibition of monopolies and
engrossing, the publicity of transactions, the suppression of middlemen, were only so many means of
securing for the individual provisions on the most
favourable terms. Municipal legislation protected
the buyer against the abuse of speculation, and also
against the frauds and the deceits of the sellers. A
whole army of functionaries—*rewards, wardes, vinders,*
etc.—was occupied not only in watching over the
observance of the market regulations, but furthermore
in inspecting the commodities imported into the town,
and in confiscating on the spot all that were not of
the highest quality or, to employ the expression of the
texts, that were not " legal."

The commonweal of the burghers was very distinctly
the ideal aimed at by the legislation which we have
just sketched. To realize it they employed arbitrary
methods, remorselessly restricted individual liberty
and, in short, set up a kind of municipal socialism of
which we shall soon discover new developments.

Such a state of things would have been impossible
but for a conjunction of circumstances which must be
rapidly explained. Of these, the chief were the
difficulty of transport, the lack of capital, and the
strength of the burgher body. If the peasant had
had the opportunity of selling his produce to wholesale dealers, who were themselves able to export this

---

1. I borrow this expression from Bücher. See his excellent
account of the " Origines de l'économie nationale," in his *Etudes
d'histoire et d'économic politique,* translated by A. Hansay. Paris-
Bruxelles, 1901.

produce at a low price, the regulations of which we have just spoken would undoubtedly have remained a dead letter. But, by the force of circumstances, the town was the natural and necessary market for the neighbouring country. The character of the roads and the means of transport did not allow the fruits of the earth to be sent to other outlets. On the other hand, in the town itself, public spirit and corporate feeling, which bound together all the members of the urban community, constituted a moral restraint strong enough to put an effective stop to attempts at fraud.

It would not be right to suppose that the provisioning of the towns exclusively depended on supplies drawn from the immediate neighbourhood. The picture we have just drawn would be incomplete if we did not find a place in it for commerce. Indeed, it is clear that a large part of the means of life were derived from this source, at any rate in the great towns. In many districts corn, and in a great many more wine and herrings, were imported wholesale by merchants who obtained their stores either at the actual place of production, or at the ports on the coast, or at the big fairs in the interior. In time of dearth or famine— and we know how frequent those catastrophes were in the Middle Ages—it was by means of these imports that the towns, deprived of their home supplies, succeeded in feeding their population.

It is exceedingly interesting to observe that the regulations, sketched above, were not extended to this alternative means of obtaining food. Made for the local market, and able to dominate it because it was limited, they could not check trading on a large scale by their narrow regulations. They were broken

G

through, as a wild boar breaks through a net set to catch larks. Municipal legislation might succeed in preventing the baker from secretly storing a few sacks of flour in his warehouse, in order to sell them at a high price at the first rise of the market; but it found itself powerless before the wholesale merchant, who landed on the town quay several boat loads of rye or wheat. Here it found itself in the presence of an economic situation to which it was not adapted. It was defeated by capital as soon as it interfered. Capital was, so to speak, beyond its ken, and certainly beyond its reach. At the appearance of capital it yielded and left the way clear. If the town's law held its own at all, it was because capital was not yet sufficiently widespread to conquer everything, because, in short, it remained an exceptional and extraordinary force. It only exerted its power in the field of wholesale commerce, and made no attempt to bring the petty transactions of daily life under its sway. But it would be a grave mistake to forget its existence, and to disregard its effects in undermining the system of direct exchange.

III.

The Regulation of the Lesser Industries. The Crafts.

The same characteristics that we have just been observing in relation to the town food supply recur, but in a more varied and striking form, in the organization of industry. Here too we can distinguish the irresistible interference of capital, as well as the local regulation of trades.

Let us first examine the group of artisans who toiled for the satisfaction of the daily needs of the population : the bakers, butchers, tailors, carpenters and joiners, masons, blacksmiths, potters and tinsmiths, etc. Indispensable to the burghers, such crafts were found in every town. Every community, great or small, possessed them in numbers proportionate to its importance. Just as the great estate, in the agricultural period of the Middle Ages, strove to produce from its own soil every kind of cereal, so every town provided from its own resources for the current needs of its inhabitants. But further, the people of the town were not the only consumers of the goods made or prepared by the local trades. "The territory which supplied the town markets with food, served also as an outlet for its products. The inhabitants of the countryside brought to the market the means of subsistence and the raw material, and in return purchased the labour of the artisans of the towns . . . . . The burgher and the peasant thus found themselves in a relation of reciprocal dependence. What the one produced the other consumed, and this exchange took place, in great part, without the medium of money : at the most money came in to adjust the difference in the value of the things exchanged." [1]

We find then an economic system, very simple and, for that very reason, easy to control and to adjust in all its parts. So the regulations, analogous to those already noticed in connexion with the food supply, recur in connexion with local industry. The principles are unchanged though they operate in different

1. I borrow these lines from Bücher, *op. cit.*, trans. by Hansay, p. 84.

ways. Municipal socialism found its most complete embodiment in the organization of the small trades, and the work, which it there executed, must be regarded as one of the greatest achievements of the Middle Ages. It was as logical in its principles, as coherent in its parts and as rich in its details, as the finest monuments of gothic architecture, or as the great " Summae " of the scholastic philosophers.

The common weal of the burghers was here, as in the case of the town food supply, the supreme object to be attained. To procure for the inhabitants goods of the best quality and at the cheapest rate possible was the essential aim. But the producers, being themselves members of the burgher body, found it necessary to take such measures as would enable them to gain a decent living by their labour. Thus it was not possible to regard the interests of the consumer alone; the artisan also needed consideration. A double system of regulations was developed. On the one hand, factories and shops were kept under inspection; on the other hand, what we should now call labour legislation and labour organization were instituted.

In the one case as in the other, the mediæval townsfolk had recourse to the same system of severe control that we have already noticed. Men were specially employed to inspect industry continually and minutely. They were constantly on duty, in the market place as well as in the shops and workrooms. No door was closed to them. They had the right, like modern excise officers, to enter, by day or by night, any place where work was carried on. To facilitate their control, the municipal regulations compelled the artisan to

practise his trade openly at his window. The municipal authority multiplied the ordinances which the
craftsman had to observe. It prescribed for each
branch of industry the kind of tools to be employed,
the quality of the raw material, the methods to be
followed in the production of the goods, etc. Fraud,
or even simple negligence, was punished by the
severest penalties, by heavy fines, temporary exclusion
from the trade, or banishment. Above all, to make
superintendence easier, the different kinds of workers
were divided into distinct groups according to their
callings. In fact the " crafts " were, to begin with,
nothing but the framework into which the civic
authorities fitted, class by class, all the artisans of the
town. At their rise the craft guilds were in no respect
autonomous corporations. Their chiefs (deans, masters, *vinders*, etc.), were chosen for them by the
échevins, upon whom alone their bye-laws depended.
The *échevins* also drew up the bye-laws of the crafts,
though sometimes they condescended to consult them
when they were drawn up. It is necessary to add that
work was compulsory, and that a strike was considered
a crime against the common weal. In short, which-
ever way we turn, we discover the artisan cabined and
confined by the municipal power for the profit of the
townsmen as a whole. His position was altogether
analogous to that of an official, and in reality he was
an official in the service of the town food supply. It
would be difficult to advance further along the path of
socialistic regulation.

But this artisan, so carefully controlled, was on the
other hand protected with extraordinary solicitude
against competition, the eternal enemy of the indus-

trial worker. If his liberty was restricted on every side, his existence, on the other hand, was assured by the same authority that made him the slave of its decrees. First of all, he had not to fear the intervention of the "foreigner." The town market was exclusively reserved for the town crafts. Except at fair time, the external producer might not bring his handiwork within the town boundary. But it was not sufficient that the foreigners should be kept out. It was necessary to guarantee the artisan against the competition of his own trade fellows. He was consequently forbidden to sell at a price lower than that fixed by the regulations, to work longer than between the bell which proclaimed from the belfry the beginning and the end of the day's work. It was penal for a craftsman to use or invent new tools, to employ more workmen than his neighbours, to employ the labour of his wife, or his children under age, and finally, he was absolutely forbidden to have recourse to advertisement, or to praise his own wares to the detriment of another's. So far was this carried, that, at Saint-Omer, the market bye-law forbade the vendor to greet the passers-by, to blow his nose or to sneeze in their presence, lest he should by such means attract their attention to his display of goods.

It would be impossible to restrict the individual's economic liberty more severely, and yet, for centuries, no protest was raised against a state of things which, to the modern mind, seems highly abnormal and artificial. That was because it was admirably suited to surrounding conditions, and corresponded completely to the wishes of the artisans. It is obvious that they could easily have freed themselves if they had felt it to be a wearisome burden. Yet, instead of demanding the abolition of this system, the craftsmen were unanimous in upholding it. The reason for this is easily explained. Producing as he did for a restricted market, relying exclusively for his custom on the town and its environs, the worker never dreamt of the expansion of a trade system that seemed to him necessarily fixed. Each master expected to obtain exactly his share of the unchanging sum of possible profits. Economic quality seemed to all the supreme rule, and all disapproved in the same degree of the man who, whether by fraud or by his own cleverness or by greater good luck, would deprive them of their daily bread, and, seeking only his private interest, reduce them to misery. Further, those who could in any case hope to rise above the level of their own class, were very few in number. The artisans living by the local market nearly all belonged to the lower ranks of the community. As a rule, their capital comprised only their house, some small fixed income and the tools indispensable to their calling. They constituted a group of small manufacturers who sold to their clients, without the intervention of a middleman, the products they had made out of raw material bought in small quantities. The restrictions put on the liberty of each were, at the same time, the guarantee of the economic liberty of all. No one, even supposing he wished to do so, could crush his fellow. If any comrade acquired, either by inheritance or marriage, more capital than his fellows, he could not apply it to his industry, and the superiority of his private circumstances, did not warrant him in starting a disastrous competition with his neighbours. As a matter of fact inequality of fortune among the artisans seems to have been very rare. Nearly everywhere we find the same kind of life and the same moderate resources. On the whole, this economic organization deserves the epithet " non-capitalist " rather than " anti-capitalist."

The artisans' sense of their common interests completed what the municipal legislation had already set up. All these men of the same calling, the same fortune and the same outlook, were bound together by the strong bands of comradeship; let us rather use the language of contemporary documents and say by ties of brotherhood. Each trade possessed its own charitable society : brotherhood, charity, guild, etc. The comrades helped one another, provided for the subsistence of the widows and orphans of members of their club. They attended in a body the funerals of their fellows, and took part in the same religious ceremonies and merry-makings. The community of their views corresponded to their economic equality. It constituted the moral bond of that economic equality and, at the same time, furnished the best proof of the harmony existing between industrial legislation and the aspirations of those to whom it was applied.

IV.

Regulation of the Exporting Industries. Wage-Earners and Capitalists.

The harmonious relations sketched in the last section did not prevail throughout the whole class of workers. In many towns, and especially in the most powerful, we must distinguish from the master-artisans, living by the local market, another industrial group of a quite different kind. We have seen that the most ancient industrial centres of town life were created by traders. Now from the very beginning, we find these traders extending their businesses beyond local markets. There were wholesale merchants collecting natural or manufactured products in order to export them. The industry of the town was at first the chief feeder of their commerce, not, it is true, the small industries common to all the towns, which we have just been sketching, but specialized industry, capable therefore of an ever growing extension, such an industry as circumstances made possible in certain favoured districts.

Of these specialized industries, the products of which were at once spread beyond their place of origin, two were developed in Belgium with exceptional vigour, the metal industry in the valley of the Meuse, and particularly at Dinant, and, in the Flemish plain, the woollen industry. The organization of both industries presented the same form, which was in the strongest possible contrast with that of the industries working for local markets. It would be an error, then, to leave it out of account, as has generally been done in theories of municipal economics. The spectacle presented by the organization of the most advanced industrial towns is, in reality, less simple than has been supposed. Side by side with mediæval characteristics we come across some features that are almost modern. It is particularly in the Low Countries, and most of all in Belgium, that these modern tendencies stand out most clearly, and it is perhaps to this circumstance that the study of the institutions of that country owes most of its interest and scientific value.

In the first place the different range of markets explains the fundamental difference between the copper or woollen industry and the small industries. Instead of producing, like these, for the local market, they produced on a large scale and for exportation. The coppersmith of Dinant, the weaver, the fuller, the dyer of Ghent, Ypres, Bruges, Douai or Louvain, bore no resemblance to the baker, or the blacksmith, or the shoemaker. At once artisans and shopkeepers, the small craftsmen sold directly to their customers. The copperworkers and the clothworkers, on the contrary, were reduced to the position of mere industrial hands. They were not in touch with the public; their only relations were with the merchants who employed them—copper merchants at Dinant, merchant-drapers in Flanders and Brabant. It was these merchants who distributed to them the metal or the wool to be worked up, and received back the raw material in the form of cauldrons or cloth, and it was they who finally sold in the market hall, or transported to foreign lands, the produce of the labour that they merely directed. Here, then, was a clearly defined line of demarcation between the man of business and the actual craftsman. The first was a capitalist, the second a wage-earner. That the coppersmiths, the weavers, the fullers, the finishers, etc., were divided into crafts, like the other artisans, is of little importance. If the form of their classification is the same in both cases, we must not be misled about its real nature. For, in the crafts working for the local market, the tools, the workshop and the raw material, like the finished product which he delivered directly to the consumer, belonged to the worker. In the metal and woollen industries, on the other hand, capital and labour were dissociated. The worker, having no access to the market, only knew the capitalist who paid him and came between him and the unknown buyers to whom the fruits of his labour went. Direct retail sale determined the economic organization of the other artisans. The trades of the exporting industries on the other hand fed wholesale commerce, and it was only after passing through a series of intermediaries that, leagues away from the place where they were made, the cauldrons of Dinant or the stuffs of Flanders, at last came into the hands of a buyer who knew nothing of those who had made them. Direct exchange, therefore, which has often been regarded as the essential characteristic of the economy of the town, was only a part of it. By its side a place, and a large place, must be found for that much more complicated form of exchange which necessitated the intervention of capital. In short, the features that have been regarded as the characteristics of mediæval industry did not belong to the workers of the exporting industries. Anticipating to some extent the future, they already displayed, in the 13th century, the spectacle with which home industries made the whole of Europe familiar after the Renaissance. If mistaken views have been held, it is because the exporting industries were, as we have already said, confined to a small number of towns. Indeed the peculiar group of circumstances necessary for their development was not at all common. An abundance of raw material, an advantageous geographical situation, and the tradition of a superior skill, contributed from the first to make it possible for certain industrial centres to manufacture, on a large scale, exportable products whose superior quality made them readily saleable in distant markets in spite of the obstacles which municipal protection imposed on their distribution. Such were the advantages possessed in a land of rivers and harbours, like Belgium, by the copper wares of Dinant and the cloths of Flanders and Brabant. Very early both these products figure in European commerce, beside the corn of the north and the wine of France or the Rhine. The situation was, no doubt, exceptional, but it was also of very old standing. It went at least as far back as the rise of the local industries, and it would therefore be wrong to regard it as arising from a later stage of economic development. In short, in the countries where the municipal industries attained their fullest development, the economics of the town present two distinct types of industry, the small local industries, and the exporting, or, perhaps it would be better to call them, the great industries.

It is by their numbers that the workers in the greater industries are most clearly distinguished from those in other trades. Since their market was capable of indefinite extension, and their production was ever increasing, the exporting industries could therefore support the masses of men who, from the 12th century, crowded into the great towns from all quarters. Unfortunately, we do not possess any certain data before the beginning of the 14th century. But at that time it is certain that Ghent contained about 4,000 weavers, an enormous number, if we reflect that the town cannot then have had more than 50,000 inhabitants. We cannot doubt that in the great Flemish towns the artisans engaged in the cloth trade, with their wives and children, formed the greater part of the population. The equality between the different callings, characteristic of ordinary mediæval towns, was here completely upset in favour of one trade, and we meet with a situation that recalls very nearly the factory centres of our own days. The following circumstance is enough to prove it. At Ypres in 1431, that is at a time when the cloth industry was decaying, it still included 51·6 per cent. of all the workers put together, while at the same date, at Frankfort-on-the-Main, it accounted for only 16 per cent.

The crowds of workers in the great industrial towns seemed to have lived in a condition very like that of the modern proletariate. Their existence was precarious, and at the mercy of crises and stoppages. When work failed, the workmen everywhere lost all means of subsistence, and bands of the unemployed spread through the country, begging the bread they could no longer gain by their labour. Undoubtedly the condition of those employed in the great industries, on which depended the wealth of Flanders, was very inferior in stability and independence to that of other artisans. Hence arose the disorders and the rebellious spirit with which they have been so often reproached since the beginning of the 12th century, and of which, for that matter, they have so often given proof. Except in times of bad trade, the position of the masters who owned or rented the workshops, was satisfactory, but it was quite different for the hands, or labourers, employed by them. These workers dwelt in the suburbs in miserable hovels hired by the week. They hardly ever owned anything but the clothes they stood up in. They wandered from town to town, offering the labour of their hands for hire.

On Monday morning they were to be seen in the public places, in the markets and around the churches, anxiously waiting for the employers who would engage them for the week. During the week the workmen's bell (*werkklok*) announced by its chimes the beginning of their daily toil, the short intervals for meals and the end of the day's work. Wages were paid on Saturday night, properly in money, according to the municipal regulations, but that did not prevent the scandals of the truck system from giving rise to reiterated complaints. Thus the weavers, the fullers, and in general all the various groups of workers engaged in clothworking, formed a class apart amid the other artisans. They were recognizable not only by their "blue nails," but by their clothes and manners. They were regarded as beings of an inferior condition and were treated as such. They were indispensable, but there was no hesitation in dealing harshly with them, for it was well known that the places of those who were expelled or ruined by fines would not long remain vacant. More hands than were needed were always at the service of the masters. Large bodies of workmen even went to seek their fortune abroad; we find them in France, and as far afield as Thuringia and Austria.

In one point, however, and that an essential point, the workers of the exporting industries in the towns of the Middle Ages differ from the workmen of modern times. Instead of being massed together in great workshops belonging to their masters, they were dispersed among a number of small workrooms. The master-weaver who owned, or more often hired, one or two looms, engaged one or two or three assistants and an apprentice. The master received the raw material from the merchants, as well as the wages, which he distributed to his staff after having first set aside his own share. Thus the workers were not directly in the service of the capitalist. Instead of being superintended by him, they were only subject in their calling to the control of the municipal officers. But this safeguard was, as we shall see later, more apparent than real until the end of the 13th century. So long indeed as the government of the town was in the hands of the rich burghers, the interference of the local authority was not likely to annoy them, since they devised its regulations, and it is sufficient to run over the details of the taking up of the inheritance of John Boine-Broke, the draper of Douai,[1] to ascertain the lengths to which the exploitation of the working class could go in the time before the democratic revolution.

It now remains to glance at the merchant-exporters who, in the end, received the products of industry and fed it continually with raw material. However great the difference between their fortune and that of the great manufacturers of our time, they must without doubt be considered as a group of capitalist specula-tors. It is, of course, important not to form an opinion in this matter without taking account of their environ-ment. But the values to be regarded are not the absolute but the relative values. At a time when the circulation of goods, compared with that of our own days, was like a brook beside a mighty river, when a vessel of two hundred tons passed for a great ship, and when the pack-horses that crossed the Alps,

1. Published by G. Espinas in *Vierteljahrschrift für Sozial-und Wirtschaftsgeschichte*, 1904.

hardly transported as much merchandise in a year
as trains now carry through the St. Gothard tunnel
in a day, the few thousands of pounds possessed by a
Boine-Broke, a Simon Saphir or a John Rynvisch,
assured their holders a financial superiority analogous
to that enjoyed by the millionaires of contemporary
industry. No doubt it would be misleading, even
with the restrictions just mentioned, to represent them
in too modern a light. The general conditions of
economic life and, above all, the rudimentary state of
credit, assigned narrow limits to their activity. They
must only be regarded as rich burghers, profiting by
the advantage that their fortune gave them, to indulge
in fruitful operations of buying and selling on a large
scale. Many were, if the expression may be allowed,
occasional merchants; for them, commerce was only
an accessory and, in a way, an adventitious occupa-
tion. They did not dare to devote themselves entirely
to such business; they only risked in it a part of their
capital; they did not undertake either hazardous
speculations, or long continued operations. But true
as all that is, it is no less true that, compared with the
artisans of the small trades, they appear to us as men
capable of undertaking great business enterprises.
The resources at their disposal enabled them to buy
by hundreds at a time, quarters of wheat, or tuns of
wine or bales of wool. In Flanders, the majority of
them were occupied in the wholesale importation of
wool, just as at Dinant they nearly all gave their attention to the importation of metal.[1]They alone were in a

1. It should, however, be noticed that this was not their sole
business. When circumstances were favourable the importers of
wool or metal also imported corn or wine.

position to acquire those precious English fleeces, the fine quality of which assured the repute of Flemish cloth, and, as owners of the raw material of which they had, in fact, the monopoly, they inevitably dominated the world of industrial labour. The raw wool which they imported into the towns, passed through the work-shops, and came back to them in the form of woven fabrics. The profit they made on the sale of the stuffs enabled them to undertake fresh importations of wool.[1] As we have already seen in dealing with the trade in the necessaries of life, the economic liberty of the capitalist merchants was complete. Wholesale traffic in wool and cloth was as free from municipal restrictions, as industrial labour was subject to civic superintendence and control. The big merchants could buy and bring into the towns indefinite quantities of merchandise as they pleased; the associations which they formed among themselves brooked no control : no one laid down a maximum for the price they demanded of the buyer. They alone in their guilds or hansas, voluntary associations comparable to our syndicates or trusts, could impose respect for certain rules and methods. Otherwise, however restricted and ill-applied might be the growing power of their capital, it was exerted without hindrance, and its freedom enables us to understand their influence and their dominance.

1. I am here describing the primitive state of affairs. Later the wool merchants and the cloth merchants became distinct. But it is impossible in a work like this to enter into all the details of the organization of capital.

H

V.

The Economic Aspect of the Episcopal Cities.

To sum up, in the industrial towns of Belgium the population was divided into three quite distinct groups as early as the 13th century. At the top was the great capitalist class occupied with commerce on a grand scale; under them came the lower middle class composed of artisans working on their own account; at the bottom of the ladder was the mass of wage-earning workers, more numerous but also more miserable than the two other classes. This division, purely economic in origin, is found, independently of racial differences, in the Walloon country as well as in low-Dutch districts. It existed at Dinant, Douai, Lille and Saint-Omer, as at Bruges, Ghent, Brussels, or Louvain. If it be compared with the usual picture of mediæval towns, it will at once be seen that its distinguishing feature consists in the preponderating importance of the great capitalists and of the wage-earning working-men. But it must be recognized that, alongside the completely developed civic community, which we have just described, the Low Countries contained many urban communities, whose members gained a livelihood from local industry and commerce, and chiefly consisted of artisans engaged in tasks indispensable to the daily life of the commune and the surrounding country, together with a few property owners of a semi-rural character. Such is the situation presented to us by most of the small towns of the county of Hainault, the lordship of Namur, the bishopric of Liége, the counties of Holland and Zealand, not to mention parts even of Flanders and Brabant. Examples of this type are indeed much more numerous than those which we have just been considering. But their number ought not to mislead us as to their nature. As a matter of fact the towns with merely local economic relations are not examples of the earliest municipal development. Nearly all of them ought to be considered as of secondary origin, as villages or towns endowed with municipal privileges and raised to the position of civic communities on the model of the great trading centres.

A place apart must be given to the episcopal cities. There, the economic causes which produced the development of the great towns in the lay principalities, were either accompanied, as at Utrecht, or replaced, as at Liége, by factors of a different kind. In any case, even in the absence of a well developed trade, the residence of the bishop could not fail to draw within the walls of his " city " a considerable population.[1] The presence of numerous officials and important institutions gave them something of the animation and life of a modern capital. This is best seen at Liége. In fact it was not till the end of the Middle Ages that the great city on the Meuse became the hive of industry it has always been since. Until the middle of the 14th century Liége was essentially a city of priests, bristling with church towers and cut up by great monastic precincts. As its clerical population increased and the court of the bishop developed, the number of artisans necessary for the maintenance of this community grew proportionately. The incessant financial needs of the eccle-

1. Thérouanne was an exception. Its diocese was too small to gain for it any real importance.

siastical establishments soon led to the establishment at their doors of a powerful class of money-lenders who, in spite of the canonical prohibition of usury, were able to make large fortunes by means of advances at thirty to fifty per cent. Liége was, like Arras, another episcopal town of the Low Countries, a town of bankers, or, perhaps we should say, usurers. The part played by the great merchants in the Flemish cities, was there played by financiers and money-changers. The class of wage-earning labourers was entirely absent. The lower middle class was altogether made up of artisans and shopkeepers. The economic and social constitution of these cities therefore presents a peculiar character, and we shall have occasion to point out subsequently the influence which that state of things exercised on its history.

VI.

DENSITY OF THE TOWN POPULATIONS.

In the preceding pages we have often had occasion to speak of "great" towns and "great" trading communities. The meaning of this adjective ought to be defined. Greatness is relative, and that commonplace is enough to warn us against the mistake of likening the great towns of the Middle Ages to the great towns of to-day. It is evident that the importance of the towns ought to be reduced to the scale, if one may say so, of the civilization in which they grew up, and the less one is prepared to contend that the Europe of the 13th century supported as many men as the Europe of the 20th century, the more readily it will be admitted that the town population of seven hundred years ago cannot be compared with the town population of the present time. Nevertheless, obvious as this is, it has not been taken into account until quite lately. We read with astonishment in quite recent works that, in the time of Saint Louis, Ypres had 200,000 inhabitants, and that Bruges and Ghent were populated on the same scale. The question deserves serious consideration. Indeed it becomes necessary to point out that demography is perhaps the most important of all the social sciences. It is conclusive, because the data it supplies as to density of population, enable us to judge of the military and economic resources of a given society, and to approach with sufficient precision the analysis of its social conditions. Even the study of political institutions has its share in the solution of the problem. Has it not been suggested, and with great probability, that density of population is one of the most powerful elements in making democratic government possible?[1]

Unfortunately the Middle Ages have left us very insufficient statistical information. It was not till the 15th century that here and there a complete census was undertaken. Before that date, for lack of any better means of ascertaining the population of a town, we are obliged to have recourse to rolls of those assessed for taxation or military service, and to lists of members of the crafts, the religious brotherhoods, and their like. But these are fragmentary sources and, at best, only permit conjectural calculations. Certain official documents, some passages in the chroniclers, give us very precise figures. But upon examination their value disappears, and it is owing to the uncritical

1. C. Bouglé, *Les idées égalitaires*, p. 96.

acceptance of such statements that the town populations of the Middle Ages have been magnified beyond
all probability. It is easy to see that the mediæval
writers did not attribute any importance to the question
of numbers. Except in the very rare cases where they
had at their disposition definite lists, they uncons-
ciously exaggerated the figures, and the contradictions
to be found in them are a sufficient proof of the small
trust to be ,placed in them. Within twenty years of
each other, two documents attribute to the town of
Ypres a population of 200,000 and of 40,000 inhabitants.
The reality was very different. Minute and searching
inquiry during half a century proves, without the
shadow of a doubt, the very small population of the
towns at the end of the Middle Ages. It may appear
strange, but it is now established that in 1450 Nuremberg contained only 20,165 inhabitants; Frankfort in
1440 only 8,719; Basel in 1450 about 8,000; Freiburg
in Switzerland in 1444 only 5,200, etc. The case is
the same if we turn from Germany to the Low
Countries. Trustworthy documents tell us that Ypres
contained 10,523 souls in 1431; 7,626 in 1491, and
9,563 in 1506. Speaking generally, there is no reason
to believe that these populations, insignificant as they
are to modern eyes, were ever greater in the preceding
centuries. At the most this might be admitted in the
case of Ypres, where the cloth trade was certainly
declining in the 15th century. But even if we suppose
that it produced a formidable falling off in the number
of the inhabitants, it would still be impossible with
any likelihood to put the population at more than
twenty thousand men at the time of the town's greatest
prosperity. Thus, contrary to former beliefs, we

ought not to regard the town populations as rising above a moderate level. Ghent and Bruges, which were reckoned among the most populous centres of continental Europe, certainly did not surpass, even if they ever reached, 50,000 and 40,000 souls. Louvain, Brussels and Liége may have had 20,000 to 30,000 inhabitants, that is to say about the same number as Nuremberg, and many more than Basel or Frankfort.

The population of the towns seems to have grown almost continuously till towards the end of the 13th century. Up to that date the emigration of the country folk into the industrial centres does not appear to have slackened. But about the year 1300 a position of equilibrium and stability was reached. The period of the democratic government of the communes was not favourable to their growth. The political exclusiveness, which they then manifested, rendered them less liberal than formerly in welcoming new inhabitants. They opened their gates with increasing reluctance to admit new comers, and while the rural population around them became denser, the number of burghers within their walls did not increase. Until modern times their populations did not, except under exceptional circumstances, as at Antwerp, pass beyond the level they had already attained.

We shall be pardoned for having dwelt at some length on a question which at first sight seems irrelevant to the subject of this book. It is, however, necessary to devote some attention to the demographic position of the towns whose political struggles and social conflicts we are to review in the following pages, in order to form an accurate idea of their resources and vitality. It is not a matter of indifference to learn that their eventful drama was played out on a very small stage. Everybody knew everybody else in the " great towns " of the Middle Ages, and party strife was intensified by personal rivalries and quarrels. The personal identity of the individual was not in those days lost in a nameless crowd. Each individual man with his passions and interests appeared in the full light of day. There was nothing abstract or theoretical about politics. It was not a fight for a programme : the adversaries met face to face and marched against each other as foes. Political convictions, sharpened by personal antipathies, were easily exasperated to the point of ferocity.

Yet we can understand the energy and vigour such a situation would impart to these men. Watched and spied upon by his neighbour, the burgher of the Middle Ages felt within himself a personal sense of dignity and a personal sense of responsibility. Each man became conscious of his own worth. If he were without pity for his adversary in times of strife, he also knew how to do his duty to the utmost when the interests of the town were at stake. If the need arose he was ready to lay down his life for his town. Though the population of the mediæval communes may be compared with our smaller modern towns, their energy recalls the cities of antiquity. They contrast most strongly with our small modern towns, torpid with the monotony of an existence adequately secured by the state, and requiring no serious effort from its inhabitants. Each of the mediæval towns in the Low Countries depended for defence and existence upon itself alone. All the services that are to-day carried on by the power of the state, the food supply, the means of communication, fortification, had to be kept up by them from their own resources. Their maintenance called for a constant effort of will, a continual devotion to the public welfare. When we compare them with our great modern communities, the mediæval towns were immeasurably inferior no doubt in extent, wealth and numbers, but they certainly rose above them in the intensity of their activities, and in the pride and devotion they inspired among their citizens.

CHAPTER V.

THE TOWNS UNDER THE GOVERNMENT OF THE PATRICIANS.

I. Formation and Progress of the Patriciate.—
II. Character of the Patrician Government.

I.

Formation and Progress of the Patriciate.

If the form alone of their institutions be taken into account, the municipalities in the Low Countries, like others elsewhere, presented from the beginning, and always preserved, a distinctly democratic character. The political community, as it appears from the town charters, embraced all the burghers. The *échevins* exercised their powers in the name of the citizens as a whole (*universitas civium*). The town was the embodiment of its inhabitants; it constituted a moral being, a legal person, including them all without exception. Theoretically it lived under the direct government of the people and the people alone. At the beginning, indeed, no alternative was possible. Defective as is our information about the life of the first trading colonies, we know enough about it to assert that at first they recognized equality as the basis of their organization. It was not merely that their population of immigrants was composed of men differing little in their social condition. Each individual settler was

interested in the support and defence of the growing
town, and therefore necessarily took his part in the
duties imposed by the needs of the community, and
enjoyed the rights that grew out of these duties. That
state of things, however, could not last very long.
The practice of commerce, along with all the hazards
it involves, and all the opportunities it offers to the
ready witted, soon introduced marked differences of
fortune among the population. Little by little the
homogeneous body of *mercatores* split into classes,
more and more distinct from each other as economic
activity increased. The specialization of callings
tended in the same direction. The artisan separated
from the trader; then among the artisans as among
the traders new shades lent variety to the picture. By
the end of the 12th century at latest, there were workers
living by the local market, wage-earners producing
for exportation, and, side by side with them, or rather
above them, merchants dealing in foodstuffs, in raw
material or in manufactured articles. From that time
the full scale of social conditions might be seen among
the burghers, from the misery of the proletariate to the
wealth of the capitalists.

It is clear that such a state of affairs was no longer
compatible with the democratic equality which had
been in force at the beginning. No conscious effort
was required to produce this result : equality disappeared of itself, obeying the same law of evolution as
the economic community to which it owed its existence.
No change was made in the text of the charters of the
towns; no declaration of principle had to be enunciated; no new constitution had to be proclaimed.
By force of circumstances power passed insensibly

into the hands of the wealthiest. The form of government, in these centres of commerce and manufacture, inevitably changed, first from democracy to plutocracy, and then to oligarchy. That the change was inevitable is sufficiently proved by its universality. On the banks of the Scheldt and the Meuse, as at Florence, the *majores,* the *divites,* the " great men," henceforth governed the *minores,* the *pauperes,* the *plebei,* the " lesser folk."

To designate this ruling class, modern historians have borrowed from antiquity, the terms " patrician " and " patriciate." In reality the loan is not very happy. For the Roman patricians were chiefs of the primitive clans of the city, anterior to the plebeians whom they subjected to their authority both in war and religion. They thus differed fundamentally from the great burghers of the Middle Ages, who emerged slowly from the mass of the people, and whose political supremacy was based solely on the strength of their economic position. Here and there, especially in the episcopal cités, as for instance at Liége, we can distinguish among them certain *ministeriales* of the territorial prince. But the exceptions are too rare to invalidate the general rule. Even where we find them, it remains true that the great majority of patricians are only merchants who have become wealthy.

This amounts to saying that they were at the same time landed proprietors. The means of credit were, indeed, not sufficiently developed to enable a capitalist to invest his profits in anything but land or in house property. Even by the 12th century, the *Gesta episcoporum Cameracensium* show us Werimbold, the first great merchant whose name has been preserved for us in the history of the Low Countries, acquiring, as his fortune grows, ever increasing revenues from land :

> Census accrescunt censibus
> Et munera muneribus.[1]

In the 13th century almost the whole of the land of the town belonged to wealthy clans, and to this day, the street names in many Flemish towns, recall the memory of the patricians who owned the land through which the streets run.

It is not difficult to understand that the sons of these successful men were often content with the position attained by their fathers, and abandoned the cares of business to live comfortably on their incomes. The inducement was all the stronger, seeing that the value of their property steadily increased, as long as the population of the towns continued to grow, and their land was required for building. Thus there early developed a section of the patriciate, and that naturally the oldest section, which abandoned the commerce on which its fortune was based. These privileged persons, called in the contemporary documents *viri hereditarii, hommes héritables* or *ervachtige lieden,* received from the people the nicknames of *otiosi, huiseux* and *lediggangers* (idlers). Moreover, many of them still further increased their resources by becoming farmers of the market dues, of the domain revenues of the lord, or of the municipal taxes. Many again lent money at interest, or shared in the banking operations of some society of Lombard merchants.

Besides these men of property, who must be

1. *Gestes des évêques de Cambrai,* edited by De Smet, p. 125.

regarded as the backbone of the patriciate, the ranks
of the greater burghers were continually swelled by
commerce. In most of the towns the guild provided
those recently enriched with a strong corporate
organization. We have already seen that the trading
associations were very old and can be traced back to
the 11th century. At first no doubt they were open
to all those engaged in foreign trade. The more
dangerous travelling was, the more the brethren
realized the necessity of not trusting themselves
among strangers except in large companies. Further,
the primitive equality of their circumstances tended to
make the merchants unite more readily with one
another, while wandering in search of fortune. But
when the great routes were, as a rule, safely open to
travellers, and when, above all, differences of opportunity and ability had introduced among the merchants inequalities of fortune, when some were tied
down in the class of retailers or artisans, and enterprises on a large scale were possible for others, the
situation was revolutionized. After the end of the
12th century the guilds of the Flemish towns were
nothing else than corporations of big merchants,
devoted to distant commerce with England and
Germany. They only accepted as members those
engaged in wholesale trade. To obtain admission it
was necessary to pay a mark of gold as an entrance
fee, a sum beyond the reach of the smaller men. They
excluded from their ranks the shopkeepers "who
weighed at the *tron*" (the public weighing machine),
and the hand-workers, "the blue nails." If an
artisan made money and wished to be enrolled, he
had to abjure his calling, to come out of his class, to

break with his companions. Thus from that period
the guild comprised those who were at once the
richest, the most enterprising and vigorous of the
burghers. Such brethren as were ruined by commercial disasters, were soon replaced by new men
who rose from the lower ranks of the population.

The power of the local guilds was further increased
by co-operation. In Flanders, after the 12th century,
almost all the merchant companies of the coast towns
formed a general society called the Hansa of London.
The Bruges guild retained the presidency of the whole
body, but the several guilds of the other towns were
represented in the council charged with the government of the group, and the exercise of jurisdiction over
its members. In eastern Flanders, Ghent seems to
have been the head of a similar organization. We
can therefore well understand the supremacy and the
influence that the Hansa merchants must have exercised among the burghers. Not only did they possess
the prestige of wealth, not only did they provide the
raw material for industry, and work for the great
majority of artisans whose produce they exported, but
they felt themselves supported therein by their
colleagues in the neighbouring towns. It may be
affirmed that they alone in the economic world of that
epoch were animated by the strength and daring that
comes of the pride of class.

The combination in the patriciate of landowners and
of merchant capitalists in no wise prevented it from
becoming a powerful unity. For between these two
classes relations were constant and intimate. Each
patrician family (*lignage*) comprised members belonging to both categories. The former class was con-

tinually recruited from the second, and this in its turn opened its doors wide to the sons of the *otiosi* who wished to devote themselves to commerce. In a large number of cases the same man was at once a merchant and a man of inherited property. In short, although the patricians devoted themselves individually to different occupations, they nevertheless formed as a whole a clearly recognizable class. They were regarded as the most typical of the burghers; the chroniclers call them indifferently *majores, ditiores, boni homines.*

The contrast between this aristocracy of plutocrats and the rest of the town population is striking. The patricians cut themselves off from the "common people," that is to say from the craftsmen, by their manners, their dress and by their whole mode of life. By the beginning of the 12th century the time was gone for ever when all those townsfolk engaged in commerce were indifferently classed together under the generic name of *mercatores*. Difference of fortune and difference of profession separated them from one another to such an extent as to render all contact impossible. Burgher society became a hierarchy on the model of the nobility. The patricians obtruded their privileged position on all occasions. They insisted upon being called "sir" and "lord" (*sire, damoiseau* or *here*). Many held their heads the higher because they had for son-in-law some knight whose coat of arms had been regilded with their daughter's wedding portion. Their houses of stone,[1] crowned with battlements, raised their turrets and their high slated roofs above the humble thatch of the workmen's

1. The Flemish *steenen* of which some specimens still exist.

dwellings. In the militia they served on horseback. In the common prison a careful distinction was drawn between the craftsman, and the burgher "who is accustomed to drink wine daily at his table." Finally, in the city churches, pious foundations enjoined that the priests should every day recommend to the prayers of the faithful the souls of the powerful gentlefolk, whose bodies rested before the choir under slabs of stone or metal, on which the dead were portrayed in full knightly costume.

No protest was raised against this ascendancy of the patricians. The commons recognized them as lords of the towns and the name was very appropriate, since in the course of the 12th century at latest, the power passed into their hands exclusively. The direct government of the people by the people fell into disuse. Little by little the class which possessed the wealth, gave the impulse to the manufactures of the town, and had, besides, at its disposal, the leisure necessary for taking part in public affairs, monopolized the whole municipal administration. Not only the *échevinage* but also all the communal offices belonged henceforth to the great burghers. It was they who provided the collectors of the taxes, the *rewards* of the industries, the surveyors of the markets, the headmen of the wards, the officers of the militia, the treasurers of the hospitals, the inspectors of public works, etc. The government, to which the towns were subjected, was, in the fullest sense of the term, a class government. Political rights, formerly distributed among the whole population, were concentrated in the hands of a privileged minority. Moreover, the administrators drawn from that minority were, in fact, irresponsible.

I

Their management evaded all control. They did not render account to anyone. They alone decided upon the necessity of raising new taxes, of contracting loans, and of undertaking public works, whether those of a useful character or those for the adornment of the town.

It is obvious, however, that the patriciate could not consent to abandon the destinies of the town to a small group of all-powerful magistrates. The *échevinage*, being a life office, would in the long run have passed like a fief into the hands of certain families, if every means had not been taken to ward off the danger. Of these safeguards the principal was the institution of the annual *échevinage* which, after being established at Arras at the end of the 12th century, spread all over Flanders in the next few years and thence passed into Brabant. From that time every member of the patriciate might in turn succeed to the management of affairs. Indeed, their share therein became all the larger because, after the introduction of the principle of annual appointment, the power of the magistrates was considerably increased. Side by side with the *échevins* in office, we now find that a council is instituted, regularly composed of the *échevins* of the preceding year. Moreover great ingenuity was displayed in devising a system of rotation of magistracies, intended to summon the largest possible number of representatives of the patricians, to the duty of governing the town. At Liége the *échevins* for life, and the annual *jurés*, were to be drawn from the different *vinaves* of the town.[1]

---

1. *Vinave* means neighbourhood. It is the name given in the bishopric of Liége to the different quarters of a town.

In Brabant the various families of the burgher aristocracy formed groups which bore the name of *lignages*
or *geslachten*. These clans were equal in number to
the *échevins* and thus each had at its disposal a seat
in the *échevinage*. Elsewhere again minute precautions were taken to prevent the town magistracies
from being exploited by ambition or intrigue. At
Tournai, as in several Flemish towns, certain electors
chosen moreover in very small numbers from the
different parishes of the town, had to nominate the
new *échevins*. At Lille they even had recourse to the
lot, as in antiquity and in several Italian towns of the
Middle Ages, for the purpose of naming the administrators of the community. But whether the appointment was made by election or by lot, the people were
equally excluded from power. In fact, from the
beginning of the 13th century at latest, commoners
were ineligible. At first this exclusion was only
taken for granted. The documents do not pronounce
exclusion from municipal magistracies, except against
thieves, and coiners of bad money. But the fact soon
found official expression. At Bruges, in 1240, it is
distinctly stated that it is impossible for an artisan to
become an *échevin,* unless he has renounced his trade
and gained a footing in the Hansa of London. At
Alost in 1276, a regulation in set terms debarred from
the *échevinage* every man of " low trade."

Both the common people and the territorial lord
were affected when the patriciate laid hands on the
town magistracies. Indeed, from the day when the
great burghers only were eligible for office, and when
even among them, the nomination of the *échevins* was
limited to certain electors, or effected by one or other

of the methods we have just described, the lord lost all power to interfere effectively in the appointment of new members of the municipal councils. If any power remained in theory, it was a mere formality, and in practice no one paid any attention to it. In reality, under the government of the patricians, the towns were almost entirely independent of the territorial princes. The bailiff or *amman* of the prince continued, no doubt, to represent the authority of the " lord " of the land. But what could a single official do against a powerful aristocracy which, confident of itself, claimed to govern in its own way, and could always, in case he gave any real trouble, resort to bribery? As for the lord, the only policy to be pursued was one of patience or resignation. For he too was dependent on those wealthy *échevins* who administered his towns as if they belonged to them. The lord's continual need of money compelled him to depend constantly on their good offices. He could not dispense with their guarantee for the loans which he obtained from the Lombards. He often went so far as to make a direct demand on them for the sums of money which he needed, and he always got them. The great burghers were careful not to refuse him the subsidies which were the guarantee of the independence they enjoyed. They were the more disposed to do so, as their generosity cost them nothing. For since they directed the financial administration of their towns as they pleased, they had only to dip their hands in the communal purse, or, if by chance that happened to be empty, to put a tax upon the " common people," in order to satisfy the desires of the prince and safeguard, at the expense of the public treasury, the privileged position which they occupied.

II.

CHARACTER OF THE PATRICIAN GOVERNMENT.

We must hasten to add that, if in the long run the patriciate, like all other aristocracies, learned to abuse its privileges, yet for a long time it knew how to show itself worthy of them. From the middle of the 12th century till the end of the 13th, it presents a wonderful spectacle of intelligence, unwearied activity and capacity for affairs. It devoted itself to the public welfare with a wholeheartedness that commands respect. It may be truly affirmed that, under its government, the civilzation of the cities acquired the principal characteristics which were to distinguish it to the end. It devised the whole machine of municipal administration, which survived untouched the democratic revolution of the 14th century, when the patriciate itself was overthrown. It gave their final form to the various public services of the commonwealth. The most important of all, the financial system, was its peculiar work and bears high testimony to its abilities. From the 12th century it not only established a system of direct taxes : it not only combined therewith a complete system of indirect impositions, levied on foodstuffs and the chief articles of consumption, but it further laid the foundations of civic credit based on the sale of life annuities. The organization of markets and market halls was regulated by these aristocratic governors down to the minutest detail. They found means to surround the town with strong walls, to undertake the paving of the streets, to bring drinking water from neighbouring springs,[1] to construct warehouses, wharves, locks, bridges and all the equipment necessary for commerce. For commercial prosperity was evidently their first care. Under their administration we see the towns purchase the old tolls of the great lords, lay and ecclesiastical, and secure for their burghers privileges of safe conduct, and all kinds of economic advantages, not only from their territorial lords but also from foreign princes. A system of posts was organized between the fairs of Champagne, those great marts of Europe in the 13th century, and the chief communes of Flanders. To facilitate the importation and circulation of goods the rivers were deepened, canalized and provided with *rabots*[2] and *overdrags*. At Aardenburg, the canal of the Leet, and at Ghent, that of the Lieve, put those towns in direct communication with the sea. Bruges spent considerable sums to put the channels of the Zwyn in order. Even if our documents were silent, the greatest civil monument of the Middle Ages that has come down to us in Belgium, the Cloth Hall at Ypres, would by itself suffice to give us an idea of the economic vigour and at the same time of the splendour of the towns, under the administration of the patricians.

An activity so wide and various demanded a complete staff of scribes alongside the magistrates. From the first half of the 13th century such a staff was completely organized. The clerks to the *échevins* drew up the deeds recording the contracts ratified

1. I am here thinking of the reservoir of Dikkebosch near Ypres, dug in the 13th century.
2. A *rabot*, a corruption of the French *rabat*, is a movable weir intended to keep the water at one level. An *overdrag* is an inclined plane by which boats are hauled from one reach of a canal to another.

before the town court, conducted the municipal correspondence, and kept written accounts of municipal finance. And, in these municipal offices, Latin, which laymen had borrowed from the church as the language of affairs, was abandoned for the vernacular, a significant innovation, and quite in harmony with the spirit which filled the burgher communities. The oldest charter known to us in the French language is from the hand of a scribe of Douai, and the oldest charter in Flemish comes from the archives of Oudenarde.

Municipal independence, completely established by the patriciate in the purely political sphere, was not less keenly upheld by them against the clergy. From the end of the 12th century, perpetual quarrels brought the communal authorities into conflict with the chapters and the monasteries in their town, and even with the bishop of the diocese. It was all very well to thunder excommunications and interdicts against the authorities. That did not alter their attitude in the least. If they yielded for the moment, it was only to return immediately to the attack. In case of need they did not hesitate to compel the priests to sing mass and administer the sacraments. Though full of respect for religion and the church, the burghers, by way of compensation, treated the local clergy with an astonishing lack of ceremony. At Liége they lived in a state of perpetual strife with them. The communal tax to pay for the fortification of the town, from which the clerks claimed exemption by reason of their franchises, produced a long train of riots and conflicts. Elsewhere the burghers tried to compel the religious houses to close the cellars where they retailed, free of duty, the produce of their own vineyards or the surplus of their store of wine. The encroachments of ecclesiastical jurisdiction were no less fiercely opposed. In the 13th century Bruges carried on with extraordinary obstinacy a long and costly suit to uphold its rights in this respect against the bishop of Tournai. No expense was spared. At great cost voluminous opinions were obtained from the lawyers of Paris; they went so far as to send to Rome lawyers charged with the duty of setting before the pope the claims of the town. But it was the question of the schools that finally brought the clergy into collision with the municipal power. It became particularly acute at Ghent at the end of the 12th century and there it was settled in favour of the burghers. In spite of the protests and complaints of the abbot of St. Peter, the *keure* in 1192 gave anyone the right to open a school. In all the great towns of Flanders, at any rate in the 13th century, though higher education remained in the hands of the church, elementary education appears to have been completely free.

We must, however, be on our guard against a possible misconception. When we speak of educational quarrels in the Low Country towns of the Middle Ages, we must define our terms exactly and not attribute to the strife a dogmatic or philosophic character. The matter in dispute was not at all the religious spirit of the instruction. On that point there was no difference of opinion. The sole question at issue concerned the monopoly of the right to teach claimed by the clergy. In the great merchant cities, large numbers of children thronged the schools, to acquire the knowledge indispensable for the pursuit of a commercial career: reading, writing, a little arith-

metic and bad Latin. Hence the quite natural interference of the municipal authority. In contesting the
church's exclusive claim to teach, it simply wished
to prevent it from monopolizing the profits of a
profession which had become lucrative, and also, no
doubt, to provide the younger generation with masters
more in touch with their needs than clerks, who were
strangers to the practical needs of existence, could
possibly be.

It is unnecessary to insist at greater length on the
civilization of the cities in the age of the patriciate.
We have said enough, and our aim has been attained,
if we have succeeded in showing what the great
burghers achieved, in bringing the towns of the Low
Countries to the degree of power and wealth at which
we find them, at the end of the 13th century. If the
foundation of the first civic communities was due to
the immigrants who came to seek their fortunes there,
in the time of the industrial renaissance of the Middle
Ages, their definite organization and their administrative system is the work of the wealthy class which,
as we have seen, quickly arose among them. But that
class did not limit its energies to politics and administration. It also devoted its wealth liberally to the
increase of the public welfare. That Werimbold,
whom we have recently had occasion to mention, is
praised by the chronicler of Cambrai for having
bought up with his own money an oppressive toll
which was levied at one of the gates of the town. The
establishment of the town hospitals again bears
eloquent witness to that mingled impulse of Christian
compassion and local patriotism, by which the merchant aristocracy was moved. From the end of the

12th century the charitable foundations instituted by it multiplied with astonishing rapidity. In the town of Ypres alone hospitals were set up in 1230, 1276, 1277, and 1279, either by *échevins* or by their widows. And just as the choir of Saint John at Ghent,[1] the halls at Ypres and Bruges, and the canal of the Lieve, still recall the lavish magnificence of the patrician government, so the property of modern Belgian charitable associations consists, to a large extent, of the donations of those men of property and of those merchants, who devoted, without stint, to the relief of the poor and the sick the wealth which the sale of cloth and wool had caused to flow into their coffers.

1. Now the cathedral of Saint Bavon.

CHAPTER VI.

THE RISE OF THE COMMONS.

I.

DECLINE OF PATRICIAN RULE. FIRST RISINGS OF THE COMMONS.

A class domination may satisfy public opinion for
many years and render the body politic services which
make it acceptable to everybody. But there always
comes a moment when the public interest conflicts
with the private interest of the dominant group, and
the harmony that has governed the relations between
the ruling minority and the subject majority, disappears. The more the latter have left the lead to
the former, the more they come to regard them with
distrust, dislike and at last with hatred. Those in
power are looked upon merely as oppressors. And
when further their privileged position does not rest
upon any legal basis and is solely the result of the
play of circumstances, fate ordains that it shall be
surrendered or abolished.

The urban patriciate illustrates this rule with

125

peculiar clearness. From the end of the 13th century its work was manifestly accomplished. Henceforth it sought only to defend a position which it felt to be threatened. It obstinately refused the smallest concessions. The spirit of bold radicalism, of which it had given so many proofs, gave way to the narrowest exclusiveness. It was transformed into a party jealously conservative. Moreover, as it grew old, it lost its vigour and its earlier adaptability. It fell into the error of most privileged bodies. Little by little it tried to exclude new blood. The clans, who disposed of the *échevins'* seats, were unwilling to admit outsiders to a share. Wealth alone was not enough to open the door to office. Monopolists of power regarded it as a kind of family possession. Henceforth birth mattered more than any other social condition. At first a plutocracy, the government became in the long run an oligarchy.

Nowhere does the transformation that took place appear more clearly than in the town of Ghent. There the *échevinage* had passed in the course of the 13th century into the power of a selfish and arrogant clique. The principle of annual change in the communal offices, though outwardly respected, was in fact violated with impunity. A rota was introduced which had as its result the retention of power in the hands of the same individuals. Each year thirteen new *échevins* (*échevins de la keure*) took office; but side by side with them the thirteen *échevins* of the preceding year (*échevins des parchons*) and the thirteen *échevins* of the year before that (*vacui;* unemployed) still remained associated in the administration. Thus was formed the famous college of the XXXIX, in which, every three years, the same men reappeared in the same places under the same names, not a single one of whom had at any moment lost his share in the government of the commune. Nothing changed but the titles by which in successive years they held office. Thus the town found itself in reality abandoned to the administration of thirty-nine life magistrates, one might almost say, to judge from the complaints laid against them and the hatred that they aroused, of thirty-nine tyrants. It is at any rate certain that at the end of the 13th century the abuses of power with which they were charged were intolerable. They perpetrated revolting injustices; they were even accused of having allowed their kinsmen to abduct with impunity the daughters of rich burghers and their retainers those of the middle class. There was nothing they did not tolerate among themselves. They left in office men who were old, sick and even lepers, incapable of rendering the least service to the state.

No doubt we cannot infer that there were such crying abuses everywhere. Still it is certain that oligarchic tendencies gained ground little by little in all the towns. From year to year the unpopularity of this form of government grew. A crowd of rich burghers, shut out from the service of the commune, contemptuously treated by the ruling *échevins* and uneasy at the dangers to their own interests, which arose from the irresponsible action of the magistrates, desired only to shake off the yoke that weighed upon them. And if the excluded rich found their burden heavy to bear, what a crushing weight it must have been for the commons!

It was the mass of the artisans who suffered most from the exclusiveness and the injustice of the *échevinage*. The very organization of the industrial police, which subjected the worker to the rigid superintendence of the municipal officers, assigned him his craft, controlled the exercise of his calling and regulated the price of his wares, was only tolerable so long as he had complete confidence in those who wielded that power. As soon as the workman suspected his rulers, he saw in their interference only an arbitrary usurpation. He did not mind surrendering his liberty in the interests of the common good and of economic equality, but he had no intention of giving it up to administrators who were obviously only governing in the interests of a caste. Thus, from the second half of the 13th century, the crafts no longer bore without complaint the patrician deans, *jurés* or *vinders* whom the *échevinage* placed at their head. Each of the crafts was eager to gain self-government, to regulate its own affairs according to its own ideas, and to take a direct share in industrial legislation. In a word, the craft was resolved only to obey those regulations on which its opinion had been taken, only those which corresponded to its needs, the execution of which had been entrusted to men of its own choice. All were agreed on the end to be attained. The cause of each trade was that of every other, and in each trade the condition of the artisans was plainly the same. Thus a single impulse led all the crafts towards the vigorous realization of their ideal.

Powerful as this movement was among the workers for the local market, it was still more intense and formidable among the wage-earners of the greater industries. It was not merely the superiority of numbers that assigned to the coppersmiths of Dinant and to the weavers, the fullers and the other workers in wool in the towns of Flanders and Brabant, the leading part in the democratic uprising which was at hand. All that we know of their social condition clearly destined them everywhere to take the initiative and to assume the control of this movement. Besides all the motives for discontent which moved the lesser trades, they had others even more powerful. Was it not the *échevinage,* that is to say the hereditary power of certain families of great merchants, which regulated their wages without appeal? Did they not see a number of the masters who employed them, assured of impunity because they themselves or their relatives sat on the judgment seat of the town, scandalously abusing their position to exploit the workers, either by withholding part of their pay, or by cheating them over the quality and the quantity of the raw material that they handed over to them? If we add to this the exclusion of the manual workers from the guild and from the sale of cloth, the superintendence of the wool crafts, which was in the hands of the wholesale merchants alone, and the peculiar strictness of the municipal ordinances regulating the textile manufactures, it is easy to understand the exasperation felt by the workers in cloth against a government which they deemed responsible for all their woes. Incapable of comprehending the function of capital in commerce, they naïvely imagined that the overthrow of the patrician rule would bring them the economic independence which they saw enjoyed by the other artisans around them. They

attributed the austerity of their circumstances, their
dependence on the scanty wage to which they were
reduced, the stoppages from which they suffered when
the export of wool was interrupted, to the injustice
and the heartlessness of the great burghers. In the
confinement of their workrooms they had dim visions
of a state of affairs very different from the existing
reality, a state in which the beautiful cloths, which
they themselves toiled to make and finish, would be
sold by them in the town market-place for ready
money, and would no longer secure the hated merchants their scandalous profits.

Coarser and more brutal than the other artisans and
also more eager for change, like all those who are
driven by the misery of their lot to live upon hope,
the cloth workers had already on several occasions in
the course of the 13th century manifested disquieting
symptoms of their unrest and discontent. In 1225
there reached the confines of Flanders and Hainault
an impostor personating Count Baldwin, who had
mysteriously disappeared in the East after having
worn the imperial crown at Constantinople for some
months. He had only to shew himself in the great
towns to win over the masses of the workers. All the
poor, with the fullers and weavers at their head, were
seized with enthusiasm for the poor emperor despoiled
of his goods and as miserable as themselves. He was
for the moment a sort of monarch of the plebs and all
but provoked a social revolt. The Countess Joan,
dismayed by the sudden explosion, fled for refuge to
Tournai. Valenciennes was the scene of serious
events. The patrician magistrates were deposed, the
men of the crafts took the oath to the commune and

laid hands on such of the rich as had not had time to escape. The rebels were not reduced to order till the town was besieged. For the rest, the whole agitation died away as quickly as it had sprung up. The self-styled emperor was unmasked; he was only an adventurer named Bertram of Rains. He was hanged and the illusion which, for a moment, he had conjured up before the eyes of the workmen of the towns, disappeared with him. Nevertheless that short-lived episode was not entirely without result. For the first time it had revealed to the workers the possibility of a change. From that moment Flanders was continually in a ferment. These disturbances became more serious as the 14th century approached.

It was in the Walloon towns that the trouble first became acute. At Douai it showed itself after 1245 by disturbances that bear the name of *takehans* and were clearly nothing less than strikes. At once the movement spread to the Flemish-speaking districts. In 1274 the weavers and fullers of Ghent were foiled in attempting an attack against the *échevins*. After this they adopted the curious method of organizing a secession of the industrial plebs. They left the city in a body and retired to Brabant. The feeling roused by that desperate resolution has left traces to our own times. The oligarchs at once besought their patrician colleagues at Louvain, Brussels, Antwerp, not to take the fugitives under their protection, and the archives of Ghent still preserve the replies which were sent to calm their fears.

Such an episode shows sufficiently the point which the feeling of exasperation had reached. But the greatness of the peril only stiffened the resistance.

J

From the middle of the 13th century onwards the communal bye-laws of the industrial centres abound in texts which are significant in this respect. The weavers and fullers were forbidden to carry arms, nay even to go out into the street bearing the heavy tools of their calling. They might not meet more than seven at a time, nor assemble for any other purpose than the good of their craft. If they began a strike, the severest punishments, such as banishment and death, were ruthlessly meted out to them. After 1242 we find treaties concluded between towns stipulating for the extradition of fugitive artisans suspected or capable of conspiracy. The Hansa of the seventeen towns, that vast association of manufacturing centres formed at the beginning of the 13th century, seems to have lost any other object except to uphold the interests of the patrician government against the claims of the workers.

The workmen's demands were the more dangerous because, in resisting the patriciate, the commons were not isolated. We must guard against the idea that all the social forces of the time were in close alliance with the great burghers and helped them to defend their cause. The mediæval world was split into too many different groups, unfriendly to one another, for a defensive league to be concluded between all those who had privileges to guard. The danger that threatened the men of hereditary estate and the merchants of the towns, did not alarm the church, the nobility or the princes. On the contrary, they profited by it to undermine the power of the proud patricians, who had shown so little regard for clerical franchises, feudal rights, and the prerogatives even of their own territorial lords. However strange it may appear to a modern, it is certain that privileged groups more than once took the side of the people. At Liége the cathedral chapter openly supported the crafts against the *échevins*. In Flanders the Countess Joan and subsequently the Count Guy of Dampierre showed them marked goodwill. No doubt in acting thus they were only applying the time-honoured principle : "the enemies of our enemies are our friends." Their ill feeling against the patricians sufficiently explains their conduct. But the artisans found more disinterested protectors. Already in the 12th century certain popular preachers, followers of those mystical tendencies which traverse in a broad stream, midway between orthodoxy and heresy, the whole religious history of the Middle Ages, had exalted Christian humility and condemned wealth in terms which were to stir men's souls in a singular manner. Such, for example, were Lambert the Stutterer at Liége and William Cornelius at Antwerp. The friars minor, whose order spread with great rapidity through all the towns in the course of the 13th century, were also to show the warmest sympathy for the miserable crowd. The spirit of the *poverello* of Assisi was carried by their lips to the poverty-stricken masses. If the Franciscans preached resignation to the people, they spoke also of justice. By shewing them the glory that awaited the poor in the Kingdom of Heaven, the mendicant preachers took their share in making the plutocratic rule of the patriciate yet more odious. More than one of them must have used his influence at the court of the count or bishop in favour of reforms hostile to the oligarchy of the town. We know that the guardian of the Franciscan convent at Ghent had some little share in the temporary abolition of the famous magistracy of the Thirty-Nine by the countess Margaret in the year 1275.

Thus towards the end of the 13th century everything combined to produce a fierce conflict. Causes economic, political and religious, precipitated the catastrophe. It came almost simultaneously in the different districts of the Low Countries. Only the small towns remained unaffected by the crisis, for in them the patriciate had had no chance of establishing itself and, social contrasts being less marked, class hatred had been unable to do its work. The democratic revolution spared Hainault with the exception of Valenciennes and Maubeuge, and the Low Countries of the north with the exception of Utrecht. But it spread over the bishopric of Liége, over Flanders and Brabant, with a violence, an abundance of dramatic surprises, an energy and a persistence, only paralleled in the municipal republics of Italy.

It is impossible to tell the story in detail here. We will confine ourselves to a sketch of the chief features in the two countries where its nature can best be appreciated and the modifications due to circumstances can best be observed : the principality of Liége and the county of Flanders.

II.

The Democratic Movement in the Bishopric of Liége.

It was in the middle of the 13th century that the struggle between the " lesser " and the "greater folk" broke out in the towns of the bishopric of Liége. It was to continue with stubborn ferocity for more than a century, and only ceased with the complete victory of the former. We have very little information about its earlier episodes. In 1253 Henry of Dinant, a patrician belonging to a rich family of bankers, profited, it appears, by a quarrel between the bishop and the men of Liége to organize a rising of the crafts and to give them a place in the government of the " city." His efforts failed. But, in the following year, the working coppersmiths of Dinant took up arms in their turn, shook off the power of the *échevins,* claimed the right to administer their own concerns, provided themselves with a bell and a seal, and in short constituted themselves a self-governing corporation. Part of the population, without any doubt the manual workers, pronounced in their favour; another part, evidently the " good folk within the town," that is to say the merchants, resisted them. Finally the bishop of Liége had to come and besiege Dinant before order was re-established there. The coppersmiths had to renounce the advantages they had gained and the patrician government was re-established. From that moment it was never free from attack. During the whole of the second half of the 13th century the towns of the principality lived in a permanent state of agitation. At Huy and at Saint-Trond the weavers were at strife with the guild of drapers; at Dinant the coppersmiths strove to recover the position which they had lost; at Liége disturbances broke out on every opportunity. Still these spasmodic efforts, undertaken without any predetermined understanding and provoked by accidental causes, came to nothing. But when, at the beginning of the 14th century, the news

of the " Matins of Bruges "[1] reached the banks of
the Meuse the artisans, roused by the victory of their
Flemish brethren, rose everywhere in revolt with the
same spirit.

This time the movement was too formidable to be
resisted successfully. In particular the course of events
in Flanders was so dangerous that the patricians of
Liége were obliged to bow before the storm. Moreover, the chapter made common cause with the craftsmen. The *lignages,* with what grace they could,
consented to share their power with the " lesser folk."
The crafts gained the right to give the town one of
its two masters and to be represented in the council
(1303). But these concessions were not destined to
last any longer than the fear that gave rise to them.
Soon the " great folk " plucked up their courage
again. Relying on the support of the bishop, as the
people relied on that of the chapter, they aimed at
restoring their ancient privileges in all their fullness.
Exasperated by the resistance they encountered, they
decided to risk all upon a single cast. They called
the count of Looz to their rescue, allied themselves
with the gentry of the Hesbaye, and on the night of the
3rd or 4th of August 1312, made a sudden attempt to
possess themselves of the city. Under cover of dark-
ness a pitiless struggle began in the streets. Little
by little the adherents of the *lignages,* overwhelmed
by the numbers of the artisans, were reduced to the
defensive. Then they retreated slowly, fighting all
the way, to the upper town and barricaded themselves
in the church of St. Martin. The sanctity of their
refuge could not protect them. The building was

1. See pp. 146-7.

fired and soon the vanquished were buried under its smoking ruins.

It was the turn of the " lesser folk," all-powerful after such a victory, to requite the intolerance of their enemies by an equal intolerance. The peace of Angleur, sealed on the 14th of February 1313, annulled the political power of the patriciate. Henceforth, membership of a craft was a necessary qualification for a seat in the magistracy. The urban constitution, formerly oligarchic, now became purely popular. The exclusiveness of the crafts took the place of the exclusiveness of the great families.

It was not to be expected that calm would follow such a drastic use of victory. The chapter of St. Lambert, the former ally of the " lesser folk," soon abandoned them. The bishop Adolph de la Mark put new life into the opposition to them. Indeed, the " lesser folk " had no sooner obtained power, than they showed themselves just as hostile as the patriciate had been to the prerogatives of their prince, and just as determined not to consider any interest, save that of the municipality, in all relations of life. At Liége, as in all the " good towns," they thought that every-thing fell within their authority. They expelled the bishop's officers, took possession of his revenues and usurped his legal functions. To increase their influence and to fill up the ranks of their troops, they allowed a number of men from the country districts to enroll themselves in the commune, and, under the name of foreign burghers, (*bourgeois forains*) to live under their protection and thus evade the authority of their lords.

The narrow policy of the towns, which had been

made a reproach against the patricians, continued, but with greater vigour and boldness, under the government of the artisans. There was soon a complete and lasting breach between them and the allies who had helped them to their victory. The prince, the chapter, and the nobility leagued themselves with the patricians against them. It was only after a long and bloody war that the crafts were compelled to sue for peace. In the end, the victors understood well that there could no longer be any question of re-establishing the former oligarchic system, since no one outside the *lignages* had any wish to revive it. The conditions, imposed on the men of Liége after the battle of Hoesselt (1328), in no degree abolished equality of political rights and did not revive any of the prerogatives of the great burghers. It was held sufficient to abolish the direct government of the town by the crafts. During the troublous years just passed, the crafts had enjoyed the direct and uncontrolled exercise of every municipal function. All important decisions had been referred to their good will and pleasure; their governors had usurped the functions of the magistracy. The peace of Jeneffe (1330) put an end to that state of things. Authority was again entrusted to the town masters (*maîtres*), the *jurés* and the councillors who alone, heretofore, had the right to convoke the full assembly of the burghers. The crafts ceased to be political bodies. The town council was for the future composed of twenty-four persons, chosen from the six *vinaves* of the city. For the rest, the exclusive preponderance of the artisans was broken. All the offices were divided equally between the *grands* and the *petits*.

It is certain that this organization was not a measure of violent reaction, contrived by the victors for their own exclusive benefit. We can clearly detect an intention to establish an equilibrium in the institutions of the city by making the two divisions, into which the population was divided, work together on an equality. Nevertheless the decree could not but disappoint the expectations of its authors. After having tasted the strong flavour of political life, the crafts could not consent to sink into the position of mere industrial corporations. Moreover, the patriciate of Liége had become incapable of fulfilling the part formerly assigned to it. Shorn of its ancient power by the events of 1312, it had been unable to repair its losses and to recruit its energies. For the *lignages,* of which it was composed, were not engaged in foreign trade like those of the manufacturing towns. The Lombards, who had established themselves in the Low Countries since the middle of the 13th century, and had soon monopolized the banking business, had diverted to themselves what had been the richest source of wealth to the patricians. The *lignages* now consisted of a small group of landed proprietors, who were more and more inclined to withdraw from municipal politics and to become absorbed in the lesser nobility. How could a class, so lamentably weakened, hope to maintain the balance of parties? It saw at once that its influence was lost and it made no effort to recover it. The crafts saw the collapse of the patriciate still more clearly. In 1331 they began a fresh agitation, and the uncompromising attitude, which the bishop now adopted against them, had no more permanent result than the moderation of the preceding year. The malcontents did not lay down their arms, and after some lingering warfare they achieved their desires in 1343. The "Letter of St. James" granted them almost all the points of their programme. It declared the "governors" of the crafts eligible for the council, left the election of *jurés* to them, and ordered that henceforth a general assembly of the burghers must be summoned upon the demand of two or three crafts. After such concessions the division of offices between the patricians and the artisans was an illusory safeguard. It existed, however, for another forty years, but in 1384 the *lignages*, whose decadence had steadily become more marked, voluntarily renounced their rights.

From that date the crafts were the exclusive masters in the municipal constitution. Only those whose names were inscribed on their rolls enjoyed political rights. The council, recruited from among their members, and no longer elected as heretofore by the *vinaves*, was simply the instrument of their will. All important questions had to be submitted to the consideration of the thirty-two crafts and settled in each of them by resolutions called *recès* or *sieultes*. The most remarkable point about this system, the most democratic that the Low Countries have ever known, is not so much the principle of direct government, as the absolute equality that it established between the thirty-two societies to which it owed its origin. It put them all on the same level and gave an equal voice to each of them. To understand so simple a scheme for the distribution of power, it is sufficient to recall what we have said above about the economic and social position of the city of Liége. In that town of small burghers, where no industry exercised a preponderating influence, all the corporations claimed, and were granted, identical rights. It would be a grave mistake to attribute, as Michelet does, this spirit of equality to a democratic sentiment peculiar to the Walloons. It is simply explained by the circum· stances of their environment. So true is this, that we find the same system adopted again in all essential features at Utrecht, another episcopal town, which differed from Liége in the speech of its inhabitants, but resembled it closely in its social constitution. There too the crafts dominated the municipal govern· ment and their *oudermannen* sat on the council, whose members the crafts themselves chose. It is, moreover, clear that the participation of all alike in the affairs of the state quickly developed a democratic spirit among the people at Utrecht as at Liége, and in Liége, at any rate, this spirit long survived the Middle Ages. The sentiment of political equality is perhaps the most lively of all the social sentiments. We shall find ample confirmation of that fact as we trace the history of its manifestations until the end of the 17th century.

The spirit of equality found less room to work out its effects in the other towns of the bishopric of Liége than it did in the capital. In most of the smaller towns one branch of industry—clothworking at Huy and Saint-Trond, at Dinant the working of copper— outdistanced all the others, gave to one group of workers the ascendancy of numbers, and brought about the existence of a class of rich merchants. Consequently, in these centres, where social distinc· tions were more clearly marked and natural differences

were greater, it was impossible to introduce a system
of complete equality. Here again the form of the
constitution was determined by the economic conditions of the place. This is particularly obvious in the
case of Dinant, the most active of the towns on the
Meuse. There the municipal government was, from
the middle of the 14th century, divided between three
different elements of the population. It belonged as
to one-third to the " good folk within the town," that
is to say to the exporting merchants, one-third to the
great craft of the coppersmiths, and one-third to the
nine small crafts comprising the mass of the artisans
of the district. This type of organization was not in
any way peculiar to Dinant. It suited the circumstances of all the towns where divergent interests stood
face to face. Accordingly, it became necessary to
assign to each of these interests a weight in public
affairs proportional to its importance. This system
is found in operation in nearly all the towns of
Brabant and, at any rate during the periods of calm,
in Flanders.

III.

The Democratic Movement in Flanders.

It was not for chronological reasons that we
described the democratic movement in the bishopric
of Liége before examining the corresponding
development in Flanders. On the contrary, we
have had occasion to see that, at the beginning of the 14th century, Liége was profoundly
influenced by what took place in Flanders. But the
phenomena which appear on the banks of the Meuse,
are much simpler than those to which it gave rise in

the basin of the Scheldt. There the forces at issue were much greater, the interests at stake were much more important and above all the conflict was complicated by grave questions of foreign policy, which exercised a preponderating influence on its vicissitudes.

From the reign of Philip Augustus, French policy had to face a Flemish question. One of the aims, pursued by the French kings with the greatest persistence, was the union with their crown of the great county which comprised the northern territories of the monarchy and offered such an admirable base of operations against England. The struggle began when Philip of Alsace (1157—1191) was count of Flanders. It was at first nothing more than one of those duels so common in the Middle Ages between an overlord and one of his great vassals. But there came a moment when the towns were involved. The power they had acquired was so great, and the interests of their commerce were so closely bound up with the policy of their prince, that they could not remain simple spectators of a conflict so nearly touching their welfare. Yet it was not a feeling of nationality, a sentiment unknown to the heterogeneous society of the Middle Ages, that urged them on. Their conduct was always inspired by the municipal exclusiveness inherent in those vigorous selfish little worlds and discoverable in the communes of all countries.

The entrance of the towns upon the stage dates from the reign of the countess Margaret (1244—1278). Threatened by the artisans, above all by the wool workers, and disturbed by the sympathy which the princess shewed the craftsmen, the patricians of the great towns did not hesitate to strengthen their position by throwing themselves upon the support of the French king. Already in 1275 the Thirty-Nine of Ghent, whose power had been broken by the countess, had appealed from her to the parliament of Paris. But the accession of Guy of Dampierre (1278) provided the burgher oligarchies with a pretext for making a formal alliance with the crown. Puffed up by the great position of his house, Guy did not disguise his impatience at the domination of the patricians over the towns. His dislike was the more dangerous because he everywhere encouraged the efforts of the commons. The king alone could save the *lignages* by extending to them his all-powerful hand. Now the king at that moment was Philip the Fair. His lawyers at once decided to profit by the situation. An alliance with the patriciate was the surest means of compelling the count to submit to the crown, and such an alliance was concluded in 1287. The *bailli* of the Vermandois became, in Flanders, a sort of royal agent, entrusted with the duty of protecting the towns against their prince. The banner of the lilies hung from their belfries, and thenceforward their magistrates, feeling themselves safe, boldly braved both the authority of the count and the impotent wrath of the crafts. The king, who in France suppressed the privileges of the communes, in Flanders deliberately constituted himself the defender of that municipal autonomy so haughtily claimed by the patrician *échevins*. Solely absorbed by the interests of the moment, the patricians were blind to the fact that Philip only supported them in order to defeat the count; they did not realize that the absolute monarchy whose efforts they were seconding against their prince, was, fundamentally, their most dangerous enemy.

The alliance of Philip the Fair with the patriciate exasperated the feelings of the commons all the more violently since the fall of the oligarchic government had long seemed imminent. The interference from outside had re-established the tottering supremacy of a worn-out and detested faction. The hatred which the patriciate had won for itself, was henceforth increased by an equal hatred for France, its champion. The partisans of France were regarded as the declared enemies of the democracy. In the eyes of the people, the lily of France was only the symbol of oppression. Accordingly the popular party gave the patricians their nickname of *Leliaerts* (men of the lilies) which they were never to lose. French influence, which till then had so deeply penetrated Flemish civilization, found itself face to face with the hostility of the populace. Owing to the action of the strife that broke out between the rich and the poor within the walls, the artisans quickly developed a kind of national sentiment. The commons took for their standard the banner of the count. The *Clauwaerts*[1] confronted the *Leliaerts*, and the class rivalries were all the deeper because they divided the town population into the enemies and the friends of France.

At first victory was with the *Leliaerts*. In consequence of events which do not concern us here, war broke out between Philip the Fair and Guy of Dampierre. It ended with the defeat of the count. In 1300 Guy surrendered to the king. Thereupon Philip united Flanders with the crown and sent there

1. " Men of the claw," because of the claws of the Flemish Lion

James of Châtillon as governor. The king made haste to visit his new conquest in person, and in all the towns the patricians vied with one another in luxurious extravagance to testify their gratitude to him.

The people of Flanders, struck down by the sudden blow, seemed resigned to their fate. But their apparent listlessness hid a fury and despair which broke out on the first opportunity. That opportunity soon presented itself. The taxes, which had to be raised to defray the expense of the welcome offered to the king, roused indignant protests. Were the vanquished, then, to pay for the rejoicings of their conquerors? The humiliation was too great; the situation became intolerable. Mad with defeat and enflamed by the hatred with which their hearts were filled, their wrath suddenly boiled over. Everywhere they rushed to arms, and everywhere the wool workers, poorer, more scorned, more embittered, than the others, but also more numerous and bolder, distinguished themselves by their violence and their audacity. At Bruges an obscure weaver, Peter de Coninc, put himself at their head, and his fiery eloquence nerved them to supreme efforts. On May 17, 1302, under cover of night they attacked Châtillon's soldiers, who had just arrived in the town to re-establish order. The cry of *schild en vriendt*[1] rang through the streets. The Frenchmen, who tried to raise the cry, were betrayed by their accent and were pitilessly massacred along with the patricians.

This audacious stroke, to which historians have given the name of the Matins of Bruges on the

1. *i.e.* "buckler and friend."

analogy of the Sicilian Vespers, changed the situation in an instant. In all the towns the commons, directed by the weavers and the fullers, overthrew the magistrates, organized themselves, appointed captains and hastily set up revolutionary governments. The proletariate of the staple industry found itself summoned, by a sudden change of fortune, to exercise the power from which the poor had so long cruelly suffered. The masses seized their chance with a brutality and a thirst for vengeance that does not provoke surprise.

Their first care was the prosecution of the war against the French. This was the more pressing since Philip, furious at the humiliation inflicted on his representative, raised an army and sent it against Flanders under the command of Robert of Artois. In the midst of the joy of victory the peril only roused the people to transports of enthusiasm. Moreover the Flemings were not left alone to face the invader. At the news of the events in Bruges, John and Guy of Namur, the sons of Guy of Dampierre, and his grandson, the handsome and brilliant William of Jülich, hastened into Flanders. These young princes boldly undertook the direction of the urban democracy, a circumstance perhaps unique in the history of the Middle Ages. They realized that the only chance left of recovering their heritage from the king was to lead into battle, and to animate by their presence, the weavers and the fullers who had been stirred by the voice of Coninc. Everywhere their presence caused delirious joy and, under the leadership of these elegant knights, reared in the French school and speaking only French, the sturdy battalions of Flanders marched against the enemy.

K

The armies met under the walls of Courtrai, and after a desperate struggle the improvised army of the Flemish towns mastered the splendid chivalry of Robert of Artois. Certainly it would be unjust not to attribute their victory in great part to advantages of position, to the ability of the young princes who drew up the soldiers of the communes, and to the imprudence of the French general, confident of cutting to pieces at the first encounter the rabble of infantry which was rash enough to meet him face to face. But the victory of Courtrai is in the main to be explained by moral causes. The Flemish artisans fought that day as the soldiers of the French Republic were to fight centuries later. They knew that on the result of the struggle depended the fall or the survival of popular government, the return of the patrician domination, or its final ruin. The class passions that were aroused gave them an irresistible might. They felt towards the French as the soldiers of Jemappes felt towards the Austrians. They saw in them nothing but the allies of an odious tyranny. The nobles, accustomed to match themselves only against feudal troops, were helpless before the sullen energy of their resistance. They dashed themselves impotently against the solid wall of pikes and halberts.[1] They never broke through the close array opposed to them.

After the battle of Courtrai, the issue of the twofold conflict which held Flanders in suspense was no longer in doubt. The county was restored to the house of Dampierre, and democratic government was firmly established in all the towns. Philip the Fair and the patricians were vanquished at one and the

1. " Goedendags.'

same time. Although in the following years the king raised fresh troops and led them to battle himself, all his efforts failed before the armies of the communes, which became harder and harder to conquer as success increased their self-confidence. At last the king had to consent to treat for peace. Robert of Béthune, the son of Guy of Dampierre, to obtain official recognition of his rights, accepted the terms of the peace of Athis (June 1305). The " castelries " of Lille, Douai and Béthune were ceded to France. In addition to a heavy war indemnity, the obligation to demolish all fortresses and to accept certain humiliating penalties was imposed on Flanders. It was evident that in consenting to these terms Robert of Béthune had consulted only the interests of his own principality. The causes of the dynasty and of the people, united during the struggle, now diverged. But the commons, who had been carefully excluded from the peace negotiations, obstinately refused to submit. Moreover, the return of the *Leliaert* exiles led them to see in the treaty, a plot hatched against them by the king, the count and the patricians. The war began again and Robert of Béthune, himself dissatisfied with the attitude of the king, ended by taking part in it.

Louis X. and Philip the Long did not succeed any better than Philip the Fair. The French troops could not cross the Lys. Everywhere they found in front of them the big battalions of the communes, and clearly they now hesitated to face them. But the troops of the towns were only unconquerable when on the defensive. They were neither sufficiently mobile nor sufficiently persistent when it came to attacking the

enemy on his own ground. They could not travel far
from their own homes, for the artisans could not long
be absent without ruining the industry by which they
lived. A new and this time a definite peace was
concluded in 1320. The territories provisionally ceded
to France at Athis were yielded to France for ever.
Flanders, till then bilingual, sacrificed its French
speaking populations and became purely low Dutch
in its language.

IV.

The Social Unrest of the 14th Century.

During all these ups and downs the democratic
system, established in the towns by the revolution of
1302, had undergone profound modifications. Though
set up originally in haste, and subjected to the influence
of the weavers and fullers engaged in the staple manufacture, who had given the signal for the revolt and
to whom their numbers lent a temporary ascendancy,
it had soon laid aside its provisional character in
order to suit the wants of the inhabitants of the towns.
There could indeed be no question of abandoning
authority to a single group of burghers to the detriment of all the others. The new state of affairs, if it
was to last, must accord a position to the merchant
class and to the artisans of the smaller crafts. Thus
we find a system of town government growing up
everywhere, which divided the mass of the inhabitants
into " members " and assigned to each of these
members its share in the affairs of the commune.
This result was not arrived at without many difficulties
and conflicts. On the one hand the wool workers did

not allow themselves to be dispossessed without resisting; on the other, the patricians claimed their ancient prerogatives and succeeded here and there, as at Ghent in 1319, in recovering them for a brief period. In short, despite numerous local differences, the general form assumed by the democratic government approximated to a system of representation of the chief interests. This was the only plan compatible with the social condition of the manufacturing towns of Flanders.

The new system was not destined to put an end to the period of civil disturbances. If the small crafts and the merchants accepted it, the one party with enthusiasm and the other with resignation, the wage-earners in no way found in it the realisation of their wishes. They had expected the democratic revolution to bring about a complete and radical change in their position. They had taken up arms and fought in the front rank with the express purpose of freeing themselves from the yoke of their employers, of attaining economic independence, and of emerging from the precarious position to which their calling had brought them. A large number indulged in vague dreams of social equality, dreams at once touching and dangerous, in which they seemed to see the unrealizable ideal of absolute justice and of the brotherhood of all mankind. Many thought that "each man ought to have as much as his neighbour," and yet the democratic revolution had not abolished either riches or misery. It might have overthrown the patrician *échevins,* suppressed the guilds and destroyed the Hansa of London; but it had not improved the lot of the industrial workers. It mattered little to them that they had won some political rights, could elect the heads of their corporations themselves and were subject to a less drastic system of law, seeing that they were still compelled to go on working without respite for their cruel taskmasters. The more splendid the illusions they had nourished, the bitterer seemed the reality. Incapable of understanding economic questions or of seeing that the very nature of wholesale trade and capitalist manufacture condemned them inevitably to the uncertainty of wages and the misery of slack times, they believed themselves the victims of the captains of industry, the cloth merchants and the whole aristocratic class of the " greater folk " (*poorters*), who, even if they had lost political control, nevertheless still compelled the commons to work for them, and still had the selling of the products of their labour.

The battle of Courtrai had only been fought a few years when there broke out among the wool crafts passions as terrible as when the artisans were under the yoke of the patricians. At Ypres the rich feared that they would be massacred by the commons of the suburbs and besought the king of France to suspend the demolition of the walls surrounding the old town where they resided. At Bruges, at Aardenburg, bloody riots broke out. At Ghent, in 1311 and in 1319, the weavers rose and the dismal tale of banishments and executions began again. Events were bound to take the same course. We can only say that during the 14th century the wool workers lived in a state of chronic discontent. On every opportunity they took up arms and only laid them down when, starved out by a blockade or decimated by a massacre, they found themselves compelled to yield to force. But their defeats only subdued them for the moment. They soon repaired their losses and with new energy recommenced the battle against those who held political power. In all the towns they acted in concert, and the signal given in one of them nearly always provoked a general rising. If they were poorer and coarser than the other artisans, they were also bolder and more violent. Further they had numbers on their side, and corporate organization disciplined their masses and gave them all the same aim and object. In each great commune their dean could raise a host of thousands of men, and treated with the magistrates as one power with another.

In all the dramatic history of Flanders under the reigns of Louis of Nevers (1322—1346) and Louis of Mâle (1346—1384), there was no political movement that the commons of the great towns did not try to turn to their advantage, and their history at that epoch could not be told in detail without recounting in full the whole domestic history of the county. After the great revolt of 1326, the weavers of Bruges directed affairs, improvised a revolutionary government relying on the peasants of the sea coast, confiscated the goods of the rich, seized the count and, finally, only submitted after the terrible defeat inflicted on them at Cassel by the king of France in person (1328). A little later, at the beginning of the Hundred Years' War when James van Artevelde had, by his alliance with Edward III, given Ghent the leadership of all Flanders, it was once more the weavers who claimed to control that celebrated tribune and to dictate his conduct. It was they who finally sacrificed him to their interests, and brought about his tragic death (1345). Under Louis of Mâle their audacity and energy attained its highest level. For ten years, and through astonishing vicissitudes, they made head against the count, the nobles and all the upper class who had something to lose. The hatred they aroused among the adherents of the established order was only equalled by the fear they inspired. But their example stirred up all those beyond their borders who were suffering and who, like them, protested against the governing class. From Liége came food; in Brabant, the artisans rose at their call; in France, above all, their success provoked the enthusiasm of the people. The rioters of the large towns made "Long live Ghent" their battle cry, and once more the king had to collect his troops and to inflict a fresh defeat at Roosebeke on the "dreadful weavers" (1382).

It is impossible to doubt that these disturbances were chiefly due to social conditions. In fact, wherever the weavers possessed themselves of power, we find them making it their chief business to hunt down the rich with ferocity. Evidently they regarded them as their mortal enemies and the cause of all their woes. But the social revolution that they desired was impossible of realization. The economic system they wished to overthrow did not depend upon the towns alone. To destroy it, it would have been necessary to turn the whole commercial and industrial organization of Europe upside down. Again, the weavers by their radicalism, concentrated upon themselves the resistance of all sorts of divergent interests. Almost everywhere the lesser crafts made common cause against them. The prince was invariably hostile to them, and the nobility, who had long been indifferent to city politics, could no longer hold aloof in face of a party that appealed to the poor and incited the peasants to revolt. At last, among the wool workers themselves, the fullers, whose payment the weavers claimed to fix and whom they strove to reduce to the condition of dependents, came to regard them as enemies and, though themselves still poorer, supported the cause of the well-to-do in order to escape their domination. The proletariate was not animated by any conviction that the poor all had a common cause. A sectional feeling alone directed them and, in the end, rendered impossible a victory for which the union of all the poor was the first condition.

But if the weavers failed in their efforts to reach an unattainable end, they remain none the less the most ardent and the most persevering protagonists of that democratic idea which so profoundly troubled the 14th century. Their chiefs, the De Dekens, the Van den Boschs, the Ackermans, the Philip van Arteveldes, and so many others deserve to be named alongside Stephen Marcel and Wat Tyler. They would have enjoyed the same celebrity as these if they had played their part on a wider stage.

CHAPTER VII.

THE TOWNS UNDER DEMOCRATIC GOVERNMENT.

I. Characteristics of the Municipal Democracies of the Middle Ages.—II. Municipal Economy under the Government of the Crafts.—III. Political Organization.

I.

Characteristics of the Municipal Democracies of the Middle Ages.

A comparison of the municipal democracies of antiquity with those of the Middle Ages proves at once that there is a very sensible difference between them. The ancient cities were absolutely identical with the state; they included all the inhabitants of the state whether they dwelt inside or outside the town. At Athens, for instance, about two-thirds of the citizens lived in the country. In the mediæval communes, on the other hand, the democratic institutions created by the burghers served no interests but their own. Their activity was confined to the immediate neighbourhood of the town and never touched the peasants of the open country at all. The governments of the democracy displayed a character as exclusively urban as the government of the patriciate had done. It is impossible to detect the least trace of that proselytizing spirit which tends to reduce everybody to one level, regardless alike of locality or legal status, that spirit which our knowledge of modern democracies has led us to regard as inherent in all popular government. It is true that sometimes the towns tried to find support in the country districts and fomented or encouraged revolts among the rural population. But such exceptional action was rare and left no permanent results. Broadly speaking, it was only by the institution of the " foreign burghers " that municipal politics to some extent penetrated beyond the immediate neighbourhood of the towns. In order to secure partisans from outside, the towns did in fact allow a certain number of foreign burghers, agricultural labourers, farmers, members of the lesser nobility, to be enrolled on their lists and to share in their privileges. These concessions granted to their recipients some right of extra-territoriality by placing them directly under the jurisdiction of the magistrates of the town. This extension of municipal rights to outsiders proved to be a very real check on the activity of the local lords in some districts, notably in Flanders and in the bishopric of Liége. In however many places these concessions may have been granted, those to whom they were extended were always a minority, and such exceptional measures in no way modified the general conditions of the people. Far from seeking to extend their law and their institutions widely over the country folk, the towns reserved them for themselves all the more jealously, in proportion as popular government became settled and developed. They even claimed, as we shall see, to domineer over the country folk, to treat them as subjects, and to compel them, by force if need be, to sacrifice themselves for the advantage of the towns. It was not surprising that they did so. In fact the divergence of interests, of needs, and of social conditions, between the country and the town made community of feeling and aim impossible. The two elements were from the beginning, and they remained for centuries, alien, if not actually hostile, to each other. Richer, more active, more enterprising and above all better organized, the towns as a rule overawed the country, and it was not till the day when political centralization had made such progress as to enable the state to subject them equally to its will, that the contrast, of which many traces still exist, began to be obliterated.

We must, therefore, conclude that the municipal democracies of the Middle Ages consisted, and could only have consisted, of privileged members. They did not, and could not, know the ideal of a liberty and an equality open to all. They arose and they grew up amid social groups, clearly marked off from the rest of the population. To them liberty always remained the exclusive property of the limited class which had first fashioned the urban polity.

We must go further than this, however, and recognize, that even, among the burghers, we should seek in vain to detect a really democratic feeling. The community of the town was made by the bringing together of smaller communities, among which all the inhabitants were divided. Each man belonged to a craft or, if he were not an artisan, to a corporation comprising those who lived otherwise than by industrial occupations. Thus the population, following the mode of life of its members, was divided into a number of specific bodies. The specialization of political life answered to an analogous specialization of work and occupations. According as a man was a smith, a baker, a mason, a shearer, a weaver or a fuller, he occupied a different place in municipal society. From the day that the crafts gained political rights, the community was broken up into separate sectional bodies, each pursuing its own interests and incapable of subordinating them to those of the rest. Naturally on many questions all these groups found themselves in agreement and aimed at the same object. But that unanimity did not result from a recognition of the general good. In every case it was some individual or sectional advantage that settled the matter. The burgher was a man of his craft before he was a man of his town, and if he had to choose between the good of the craft and the good of the town, his attitude was never in doubt.

Under such conditions there was no place for such citizens as those of ancient times. The rights and duties of the individual did not flow directly from the state. Between the man and the commonwealth interposed the group of comrades, which seized upon and absorbed him and ordained the part that he was to play, a part too which he would play the more willingly because he identified himself with the craft by which he lived. The divergence of interests that we noticed between the towns and the country, occurred again, therefore, within the towns, although to a less degree, and made impossible the development of a democratic spirit. It would, perhaps, be better to say that it gave to the mediæval democracy a character quite different from that which democracy has assumed either in antiquity or in modern times.

It was not because the theory of democratic government was unknown in the Middle Ages. The
philosophers formulated it very clearly in imitation
of the ancients. At Liége, in the middle of the civil
disturbances, the good canon, John Hocsem, gravely
examined the respective merits of *aristocratia, oligar-
chia* and *democratia* and finally pronounced in favour
of the last. It is, moreover, quite well known that
more than one of the schoolmen formally recognized
the sovereignty of the people and its right to dispose
of power. But these theories had not the slightest
influence among the burghers. It is possible to
detect their influence in certain political pamphlets of
the 14th century and in some literary works; on the
other hand it is absolutely certain that, in the Low
Countries at any rate, they had not the least effect
on the commons. The people of the towns, devoted
entirely to practical affairs, remained as much
strangers to the speculations of the schools as the
clergy were to the cares of commerce and manufacture.
Before the 15th century not one of the numerous de-
magogues or politicians whom they produced appears
to have been an educated man; many of them seem to
have been quite illiterate. The mysticism of the
Franciscans and Lollards, with its exaltation of
poverty and its condemnation of wealth, contributed
to some extent to the earnestness of their convictions.
But, if we look closely, we see that their actions can
only be effectively explained by a conflict of interests,
and that, in a word, they were only the representatives
of a single social class whose tendencies determined
the programme. No doubt it is true that their leaders
did not all come from the lower ranks of the people.

We find among them a good number of wealthy men, of patricians and even of the lesser nobility. Here we need only recall that Henry of Dinant belonged to one of the most powerful families of Liége, and that Philip van Artevelde sprang from among the great burghers of Ghent. We may be sure that personal ambition and private animosities often brought the popular party unexpected auxiliaries. But these could only maintain their ascendancy in proportion as they identified themselves with the needs and aims of that party.

The influence of individuals on the development of the democratic movement has, moreover, been very slight, and it could hardly have been otherwise. The promoters of the new state of things were, as a matter of fact, not isolated individuals but groups of men. The fall of the patrician régime was the work of the crafts. It is perhaps unnecessary to recall the fact that the craft, by the strict discipline imposed on its members, by the corporate spirit animating it, by the community of interests on which it rested, limited the part played by individual personality to a greater degree than has ever been the case subsequently. We have already[1] had occasion to make it clear that the history of the rise of the municipalities does not tell us of legislators. It is the same in the case of the democratic revolution. Our sources do not furnish us with the names of any creator of new institutions, and the institutions themselves, by the likeness they show when the circumstances are analogous, prove that they were formed spontaneously by the action of the same needs and hopes. Everywhere the artisans, suffering

1. See above, p. 56.

from the same evils, demanded the same remedies, and
wherever they had sufficient power they applied them
in the same way.

We must not fail to notice that the system established in the towns under popular government nowhere
involved the radical recasting of the administration.
The democracies of the Middle Ages, compared with
those of antiquity, were remarkably conservative. At
Athens the whole system of magistracies, the whole
of the judicial, financial and military organizations of
the state, were radically affected as soon as the people
gained power. But nothing of the sort happened at
Liége, Bruges or Ghent. There the administration of
the town remained in the hands of the *échevins* or the
council, and no essential modification of it took place.
The municipal machine retained all its ancient
wheels. It continued its work as before. The driving
power alone was changed. Instead of obeying an
oligarchy of rich men, its action was henceforth
determined by the crafts. It was rather a change of
political spirit than of political system. Nevertheless,
that was sufficient to produce very important results.

II.

MUNICIPAL ECONOMY UNDER THE GOVERNMENT OF THE CRAFTS.

Let us first of all examine the economic organization. A few words will be enough to let us understand
its character. Before the triumph of democratic
government, the crafts were under the strict control of
the *échevins*; afterwards each of them became self-
governing, exercising jurisdiction over the members

in industrial matters, and intervening in the drafting
of regulations which affected them. In short, professional corporations henceforth enjoyed the right of
managing their own affairs in their own interests.
That was the first privilege they claimed, and from it
all the others followed. To be precise, the *échevins*
did not lose all authority over them. They published
the statutes and, in the case of a quarrel between two
crafts, they brought the dispute before their own court.
But, however important these remaining prerogatives
were, they none the less left to each corporation of
workmen a complete independence in its daily life.
The deans, the *jurés*, the *vinders* of the crafts, instead
of being selected for office by the magistrate, were
freely appointed by the members. The consequence
was that their authority, now willingly accepted, was
all the more effective.

The new control was, at the same time, much more
active and much more minute than the old one. The
corporate spirit, henceforth freed from restrictions,
shewed itself in all its fullness, and worked itself out
to its logical conclusions. The lesser burghers, being
now in a position to conduct their own administration
in their own way, became uncompromising adherents
of that policy of protection which was the guarantee of
their survival. We see them continually drawing closer
the network of industrial regulation, surrounding the
preserves of each calling with higher and stronger
barricades, and watching more carefully to prevent any
competition with the local market. Commerce on a
great scale, by which the patricians lived, inspired them
with an insurmountable distrust. They taxed their
wits to evade its encroachments. They gave full scope

L

to their anti-capitalist tendencies. Manifestly their aim was to preserve for their members the monopoly of each industry. They also sought to rid the town of all strangers, or, at any rate, to subject them to a control so strict that their presence could do no harm. It was not until the rise of democracy that the peculiar characteristics of municipal economy appeared in their full development. Not only were industrial statutes from that time forward constantly multiplied, but legislation imposed on the market halls, the middle-men and on all the machinery of wholesale trade, ordinances of ever-increasing minuteness, ordinances which were evidence of their fear and dislike. Great ingenuity was shewn in the attempt to find a system which allowed the townspeople to sell as much as possible to the foreigner, while reducing to a minimum the amount which they had to purchase from him.

It was above all in connexion with the organization of labour, that the protectionist tendencies of the new government were most clearly revealed. As soon as the regulation of the crafts was put into the hands of the artisans themselves, they hastened to exploit the situation for the exclusive profit of their members. If the *échevins* had not succeeded in imposing upon them some moderation, and if the interest of the consumer had not, in due course, clashed with the interests of the producer, they would not have hesitated to sacrifice the public to their monopoly. The common weal of the town was not now, and could no longer be, the motive of their conduct. Each professional corporation looked upon itself as an independent body, the privileged proprietor of one branch of industry. It behaved exactly like a proprietor. In similar

manner it considered the craft guild as a family
property, passing naturally from father to son. It
reduced the time of apprenticeship in favour of the
sons of "masters," while making it still longer and
still more expensive for new-comers. Similarly it
raised difficulties in the way of the "brother" who
came from outside to gain an entrance. Before he
was admitted to the exercise of his calling, he had to
present a certificate in due form, shewing that his
conduct, life and morals were good, and a testimonial
to the effect that he had complied with the regulations
for apprentices in some "good town" (*bonne ville*).
Further, he was not accepted unless the members of
the craft in the town receiving him enjoyed complete
reciprocity in the town from which he came. It
sometimes happened that the terms became even less
generous, and that the gaining of the status of a
burgher was imposed as a preliminary condition of
the right to work. The later we come down, the
greater the number of restrictive measures. It was
the same with each craft as with the patriciate in times
past. The advantages which they secured, inevitably
led the crafts to reserve these advantages for their own
members, to build up a wall of privilege around each,
and to regard only the maxim *beati possidentes*.

The selfishness shewn towards outsiders had its
counterpart in the care the craft took of its members.
It spared no effort to give them security and to better
their conditions. It organized charitable institutions
and mutual aid. If its resources allowed, it founded
a hospital for the aged, and built a chapel or secured
one in some church. When a comrade died, it was
present officially at his funeral and provided for his

widow and children. The spirit of unity and Christian charity by which it was stirred is really worthy of admiration. Within the narrow circle of the calling to which it was limited, the craft could, and did, maintain brotherhood and general equality. It did not allow one master to do anything to the hurt of other masters, to take away their customers, to increase to their prejudice the number of his hands or apprentices. Moreover, the interest of the group proved strong enough to withstand the impulse of private interest and personal ambition. There were but few who sought to escape from the common rule through discontent with conditions under which they were assured of a secure and honourable living. In spite of the difference in rank, masters, workmen, and apprentices were united by a spirit of unity and concord. For though the masters enjoyed important privileges, their way of life resembled that of their assistants, whose work they shared and whom they had formerly, in the days of their apprenticeship, lodged under their roof, fed at their table and treated like their own children.

It is unnecessary to say more to prove that the crafts, as organized in the 14th century, had reached a state of perfect equilibrium. Henceforth they were not to develop further, either in numbers or in craftsmanship. Towards 1350 they reached their zenith. The position of artisans has never been more favourable than at that time. But its very advantages made them henceforth conservative and they fell into a groove. They were no longer willing to share their good fortune. Their ranks were no longer open to new-comers, and, as we have already had occasion to point out, the period of their fullest expansion was also the period at which the population of the towns became stationary.

It is evident that the growing particularism of the crafts could not but strengthen the particularist policy of the towns. Springing from the essential conditions of their town life and already in evidence under the patrician government, this narrow spirit became all the more powerful as soon as the whole body of burghers, sharing in political power, united to strengthen it. The aristocratic burghers were mainly concerned for the interests of trade on a large scale. Henceforth local trade began to be the chief consideration, as was natural when the leadership passed from the wholesale merchants to the artisans. To begin with, an attempt was made to widen the area of the ordinary trade of the town as much as possible. Each great commune imposed its authority upon a definite area of the surrounding country, and claimed the castelry (*châtellenie*) or *quartier* round about, as subject to its direction. It laid down the law not only for the villages but for the small towns in its neighbourhood. It wrested from the prince, or imposed by force, an order prohibiting the exercise of certain callings in the territory that it reserved for itself. From the beginning of the 14th century the manufacture of cloth was forbidden in all the districts surrounding Ghent, Bruges and Ypres, and upon the least infraction of this privilege, the crafts sallied out in arms and pitilessly broke the weavers' looms (*ostilles*), the fullers' vats and the frames for stretching the cloth. At Sluys, all the industrial corporations were put under the superintendence of Bruges. Ghent interfered continually in the affairs of Grammont, Oudenarde and Termonde. Poperinghe lived under the tutelage of Ypres. The right of the stronger was used without consideration and, when it had lasted for some time, it passed into custom. The commune that enjoyed it, glorified it with the name of a "franchise" or "good custom," regarded it as sacred and often went so far as to obtain its official ratification. The great towns increased incessantly the number and the range of their privileges, and secured still more immunities from the ordinary law. In the sphere of the general interests of all the burghers, they acted in the same way as the crafts had done in the more restricted sphere of the interests of their calling. Each town strove to secure the greatest possible number of monopolies. Hence the appearance of those staple privileges which assured to certain places the exclusive market for a particular kind of produce, or even, some-times, for all the goods entering a defined area. In Flanders, Bruges became the distributing centre for merchandise entering the Zwyn, and the general staple for woollen goods. Ghent obtained for itself the staple for grain. In Brabant, Mechlin became the staple for salt and fish, while in Holland the staple for all goods going by river went to Dordrecht.

It was inevitable that such advantages, favouring one town to the hurt of all the others, should soon become a permanent cause of dispute. During the government of the patricians, the dominant class, to which the maintenance of the general movement of trade and of distant commerce was, in each town, a matter of importance, had nowhere thought of securing control over them for its own advantage. Organizations, like that of the Hansa of London or the Hansa of the Seventeen Towns, show us that the patricians had sought by co-operation between towns the means of giving all the local guilds a share in the advantages of trade. Now, on the other hand, the protectionist spirit of the crafts began to dominate municipal policy. Henceforth the only salvation seemed to lie in privilege, in the restriction of the liberty of others. Ultimately the exclusive spirit prevailed, and involved every community in a perpetual strife against the rival exclusiveness shewn by all its neighbours. The hostility of Bruges and Ghent grew steadily during the 14th century. At the same period, the question of the staple set up constant strife between Mechlin and Antwerp. In the bishopric of Liége, Dinant was bent upon the ruin of Bouvignes, its neighbour and industrial rival. United action, of which the towns of the 13th century gave so many examples, is no longer to be found after the beginning of the period of democratic rule. If it still happened that several communes joined forces, it was because one of them had imposed its leadership on the others and had taken them in tow. This was clearly the case in Flanders, where first Bruges, and then Ghent, more than once reduced all the countryside to subjection, and compelled it to follow their lead whether it wished or no. In short, if popular government everywhere gave to the towns similar institutions and tendencies, yet, by isolating each of them within the narrow circle of its peculiar interests, it at the same time rendered them incapable of united effort.

However fully democratic institutions were developed in other respects, they very rarely, and it is

necessary to insist upon the point, attained the goal
at which they aimed. It was only where, as at Liége,
almost the whole active population belonged to the
lower middle class, that the full consequences of the
new state of things were realized. But in the great
centres of Flanders and Brabant the control of
economic relations never fell completely under the
influence of democracy. There, its exclusive spirit
could not have triumphed without ruining the great
manufactures. It did succeed in permeating the lesser
crafts and it left its mark unmistakably on the local
trade : commerce on a great scale remained beyond
its reach.

No doubt democracy considerably restricted commercial freedom. Its anti-capitalist tendencies no
longer permitted the rapid accumulation of those great
fortunes that were made during the 13th century. The
shameless exploitation of the workers ceased; wages
were regulated in a more equitable way, and the
workman, freed from the domination of the great
merchants, found in his trade guild a precious
guarantee against the abuses of the truck system and
the frauds and violence of which he had long been
the victim. It remains none the less true, however,
that the exporting industries, the cloth trade of
Flanders and the coppersmiths' business of Dinant,
had enough vitality to continue flourishing. Their
very nature gave them a peculiar position. They were
on quite a different footing from the rest. In both of
them the capitalist employer always remained the
entire master over the workers, who were never able
to emerge from the condition of wage-earners. It may
well have been that some master-weavers or master-

fullers, favoured by circumstances, acquired a comfortable competence. It even seems that in the branches of industry accessory to the cloth trade, for instance among the shearers, the dressers, and, above all, among the dyers, most of the heads of the workshops occupied a favourable position. Finally, too, we must remember that the suppression of the privileges of the guilds and the Hansas enabled a good number of these more fortunate ones to take part in wholesale commerce. It is, however, certain that, after the democratic revolution as well as before, the great mass of the wage-earners continued to live in a condition very similar to that of our modern proletariate. Afterwards, as well as before, most of the weavers and fullers were unable to attain the ideal which they saw realized in the other crafts. They could not free themselves entirely from the interference of capital, slight as it had become. For its complete disappearance, it would have been necessary for the cloth dealers to renounce the export trade wherein lay their strength and to be content with the local market. Then, and then only, the weaver might have become a typical mediæval artisan, selling by retail in his shop the pieces of stuff he had himself manufactured. Moreover, there came a day when that transformation was effected. But by that day the great epoch of Flemish industry was past and there remained only the memory of its ancient activity.

III.
POLITICAL ORGANIZATION.

The description just given of the economic organization of the towns under popular government was indispensable for the proper understanding of their political organization. In spite of innumerable differences in detail, this presents everywhere the same general characteristics. In principle it reverts to that direct government which had been practised at the beginning during the childhood of the communes. But its activity assumed a new form, due to the division of the inhabitants into a number of distinct corporations. No one was qualified to have a voice in the administration of the town by reason of his position as a simple burgher. In order to have a share in it, he must be part of a legal group. Political as well as economic life belonged only to societies: neither was open to the isolated individual. The *jus civitatis* did not take its effect except by the enrolment of the citizen in a craft or in an officially recognized corporation.

In the towns where the economic constitution was very simple, as for instance at Liége, all the crafts possessed an equal authority. But most often the inequality of the power or interests of the individual societies resulted in the establishment of intermediate links between the craft and the commune. These were the associations called " members " (*leden*), each of them comprising one or more of the craft associations. At Bruges in the middle of the 14th century, the commune consisted of nine such members : (1) The *poorterie*, that is the burghers living on their private incomes or by wholesale commerce; (2) the drapery crafts: weavers, fullers, shearers and dyers; (3) the butchers and fishmongers; (4) the seventeen *neeringen* (a group of seventeen less important crafts); (5) the *hamere* (hammer) or metal-working crafts; (6) the *ledre* (leather) or leather-working trades; (7) the *naelde* (needle) or crafts working with the needle; (8) the bakers; (9) the brokers with some other small trades. It is obvious that similarity of calling was taken as the principle of classification, although in many cases circumstances made it necessary, in order to maintain a balance between the groups, to gather into some of them stray industries of quite different types. In most of the towns of Brabant we find a similar system. At Brussels, where it appeared in its most complete form, the burghers were divided into the patriciate, comprising seven *lignages,* and nine " nations," among which all the crafts were distributed. At Ghent and Ypres, where the cloth trade outweighed everything else, it received a position in conformity with its importance. At Ypres the commune consisted of four bodies: (1) the *poorterie* with which were combined the butchers, the fishmongers, the dyers and the shearers; (2) the *wevambacht* or weavers; (3) the *vullerie* or fullers, and (4) the *gemeene neeringen,* or common crafts, comprising all the other societies of artisans. Ghent presented a similar picture. There also, by the side of the *poorterie,* there existed the " members " of the weavers, the fullers, and the small crafts. This last member included at first fifty-nine trades but later only fifty-three.

There was, however, nothing in this organization peculiar to the towns of the Low Countries. It answered so naturally to a form of government in which the crafts controlled the municipal power, that we encounter in it all its essential characteristics in a large number of the towns of Italy and Germany. Our information does not enable us to determine whether, in Flanders and Brabant, it is to be regarded as a simple adaptation of the constitution to the circumstances of city life, or whether the law of imitation is here manifesting itself, and we ought to some extent to recognize outside influence. But in any case Germany cannot have been the source of any such external influence. In that country the democratic revolution came later than in the Belgian provinces, and we even know that Cologne for instance, after the rising in 1396, adopted the constitution of Liége. It is not impossible, however, that Italy, and particularly Florence, may have inspired to some extent the system we have just described. The economic relations between Tuscany and the Low Countries were so intimate that the institutions of the one cannot have been altogether unknown to the other, and it is not rash to believe that those of Italy may, in some measure, have served as a model to some of the Netherland cities.

However that may be, the organization of the burghers into " members " clearly reveals its intention. It aimed at establishing a steady balance between the different social groups of the commune. Except at Liége, where the enfeebled patriciate disappeared as a distinct corporation, the patricians were everywhere accorded a share of the control, side by side with the artisans, and the part which the artisans played was proportioned to their importance and the nature of their industry. It is right, then, to regard the democratic constitutions of the 14th century as a very curious attempt to represent interests. They did not resign themselves, like modern democracies, to the blind force of numbers. They attempted to doctor the votes, if the expression may be allowed, and to adapt the political, as closely as possible, to the social organization. The actual groups were only accorded equal rights where, as at Liége, their difference in power was practically imperceptible. Everywhere else, whether in the Walloon country or in the Flemish-speaking districts, the economic pre-eminence of the group determined the degree of its participation in power. At Dinant, where copper-working enjoyed a degree of importance analogous to the cloth industry in Flanders, the municipal constitution recalled very distinctly the system in vogue at Ghent or Ypres. The population was divided into three " members " : the burghers " within the town," the coppersmiths and the " good crafts."

If the creation of the " members " necessarily gave unequal political power to the different crafts, in return it allowed each " member " the same amount of interference in municipal government. Minute precautions were taken that no group should have ground for complaining that its interests were sacrificed to the rest of the " members." The offices of the commune were carefully distributed among them, and rules were made that reserved to the representatives of the various " members " in turn a certain number of seats among the magistrates. But this equilibrium, difficult enough to set up to everyone's satisfaction, was even more difficult to maintain. Each type of burghers tried to get the greatest advantage possible out of it. The representation of interests is only a means for allaying quarrels; it does not end them. We find the civic constitutions subject, during the 14th century, to perpetual fluctuation. They were

continually revised; " members " were added or suppressed, the classification of crafts was modified and
still there was dissatisfaction. In this respect the
history of Ghent, the most vigorous and powerful of
the Low Country towns, is particularly instructive.

Immediately after the battle of Courtrai the commons, puffed up by their victory, set about the
extermination of the hated patriciate. As at Liége,
the crafts alone enjoyed political rights. The cloth
workers, who had so largely contributed to the establishment of the new order of things, did not fail to
reserve for themselves the lion's share of authority.
Of the three " members " into which the burghers
were divided, one was assigned to the weavers, another
to the fullers and the third comprised the whole of the
remaining crafts. The oligarchic reaction of 1319 put
an end to this organization. But, as the result of the
economic crisis, which was produced by the interrup-
tion of the supply of English wool in 1337, the wage-
earners of the staple industry rose in revolt and
re-established the government which had been
abolished.

The renewed democratic rule could not maintain
itself for any length of time. The weavers, largely
outnumbering the fullers, soon tried to make them
submit to their influence. On May 2, 1345, the two
parties entered upon a decisive struggle, and the
fullers, crushed by their adversaries, no longer formed
a " member " of the town. Four years later it was
the turn of the weavers to acknowledge defeat.
Exasperated by the oppressive predominance exercised
by the weavers over the commune, the small crafts
united with the fullers, and on January 13th, 1349, a

fresh conflict brought about a fresh change of government. The "member" of the weavers was suppressed, and the vacant place was seized by the great burghers (*poorterie*), who henceforth worked with the fullers and the lesser crafts as the three "members" entrusted with the administration of the town. By an insurrection in 1359 the indomitable weavers drove this alliance from power and recovered it for themselves. They at once seized the opportunity to humble the fullers, who in 1360, after a terrible fight in the Friday Market, had to renounce, and this time for ever, the position they had till then occupied, a position neither justified by their numbers nor by the importance of their calling.

The fall of the fullers brought about the reconstruction of the " member " of the *poorterie*. It was no doubt realized that, in a town essentially industrial, it was impossible to deprive the merchants and employers of all political influence, without seriously injuring the general welfare and also without inspiring them with a permanent hostility to established institutions. From that time Ghent never changed its type of constitution. The *poorters*, the weavers and the lesser crafts worked permanently with the *échevins* in the management of affairs. Nevertheless the influence of the *poorters* was much smaller than that of the others. The *collace*, or great council of the town, was composed of the fifty-three deans of the lesser crafts, of twenty-three *jurés* of the weavers, and of only ten patricians. Further, about 1368, an arrangement was made by the three "members" by which, "seeing that each of the two ' members ' of the crafts is beyond comparison more numerous than the ' member ' of the burghers, and in all the charges laid upon the town has sustained the greater charge,"[1] ten seats in each of the two divisions of the *échevins* were assigned to the weavers and the lesser crafts in the proportion of five to each party, while the burghers were reduced to a share commensurate with their insignificance and obtained only six.

Such was the legal municipal organization at Ghent down to the battle of Gavere in 1453. But the citizens by no means adhered to it exactly. In fact there were constant infractions of its provisions. The chief dean of the crafts and the dean of the weavers gained possession of an authority absolutely incompatible with the normal action of that proportional representation of interests which the system attempted to realize. The weavers, also, never lost an opportunity of trying to secure the controlling power over the municipality. The commune was periodically disturbed by their violent efforts, and it was only the progressive decline of the cloth trade that, from the beginning of the 14th century, impaired their ascendancy and led them, at last, to accept the partition of power between themselves and the other " members."

The situation, which we have just described in the case of Ghent, recurs, though in a less striking form, in nearly all the great towns. Moreover, even in quiet times, the regular action of the popular institutions produced all kinds of quarrels. The magistrates, drawn from among the crafts, had no power to compel

1. See V. Fris, *Les origines de la réforme constitutionnelle de Gand de 1360-1369.* Gand, 1907.

them to respect decisions of which they did not approve. At every turn it was necessary to have recourse to the general council of the commune and to appeal to it to decide disputes. But new difficulties arose at once. Each "member," voting separately, tried to force the others to adopt its opinion. It was only on the rare occasions when all arrived spontaneously at the same point of view, that a decision had a chance of being accepted. If there was a disagreement, the minority refused to bow to the majority. Each "member" obstinately stood by its own resolutions. At any moment an appeal to arms might be made; then the crafts assembled under their banners and faced one another in battle. Thus they often found themselves confronted with the alternatives of either leaving pending questions unsettled, or of settling them by a bloody conflict. This internal strife, which gives such a tragic character to the history of the great communes, was an evil inherent in the form of their political institutions, and its gravity was always directly proportioned to the degree of autonomy they allowed their "members."

We need not then be surprised at the turbulence of the great towns under democratic government. By carrying to the extreme limit the autonomy of the crafts, long held in check by the patriciate, the government at the same time made friendly relations between them impossible. None of them was ever able to rise above its group interests. It brought to their defence an astonishing heroism, but it was incapable of reconciling them with the interests of the other groups. The artisans confused, and could not help confusing, liberty with privilege. Their corporate

M

spirit overcame their patriotism. It must indeed be admitted that towns, where the popular government held the balance true between the crafts, were very rare. Nearly always the more powerful groups abused their power, and imposed their wishes on the weaker " members."

CHAPTER VIII.

THE URBAN DEMOCRACIES AND THE STATE.

I. Relations between the Towns and the Princes before the Burgundian Period.—II. The Conflict between the Municipalities and the Monarchy in the 15th Century.

I.

Relations between the Towns and the Princes before the Burgundian Period.

In all the countries of western Europe, the governing bodies of the municipalities of the Middle Ages were animated by a more or less active republican sentiment. It could not well have been otherwise. For the economic exclusiveness of the burghers, as well as their social development, necessarily drove them to achieve complete autonomy, to deal with their affairs in their own way and, in short, to transform themselves into a " state within the state." These tendencies, already very marked in the patrician period, became more pronounced under democratic administration, which in this respect continued the tradition of the government that had been overthrown. In France and England the royal power was strong enough to oppose, from the first, the efforts of the towns and later to triumph over them. In Italy and Germany, on the other hand, the weakness of the central authority condemned it to yield, and a flourishing crop of free towns soon grew up on both sides of the Alps. The Low Countries show us an intermediate position. Though the great communes reached a high degree of independence, they never succeeded, in spite of all their efforts, in completely emancipating themselves from the authority of their princes. They did not become states within the state; they remained part of the territorial principalities from which they wished to escape. Though they were the most vigorous elements in these states, though they won the first place in them and had a preponderating importance, though their autonomy and liberty of action are in the strongest contrast with the ever-increasing subordination to the crown of the English and French towns, yet they never succeeded in crossing the line. They differed both from the free imperial towns of the empire, and the municipal republics of Tuscany, and from the communes of France under the strict superintendence of the king's provosts and bailiffs.

Their power and wealth easily explain why they did not share the fate of the French towns. But how was it that they did not succeed in acquiring the status of the German and Tuscan cities? Why did not Liége, for instance, which was in no way inferior to the episcopal cities of Germany in population or resources, reach that position of holding immediately of the emperor which so many of them attained? Above all, how was it that Ghent and Bruges, which dared to provoke the king of France to a quarrel and which succeeded in holding their own against him at the beginning of the 14th century, could not shake off the supremacy of their immediate lord, the count of Flanders?

It is not difficult to answer this question.

A municipal republic did not, as a matter of fact, enjoy an absolute independence when it had thrown off its allegiance to its immediate lord. It only escaped the power of the count or bishop by putting itself under the direct power of the higher suzerain. The German town was only free in the sense that it exchanged the neighbouring and very active authority of its lord for the distant and very feeble authority of the emperor. But by the 14th century the emperor had become a foreigner in the Low Countries. His suzerainty over the countries on the right bank of the Scheldt was merely nominal. No one, either in Holland, Brabant, Hainault, or in the bishopric of Liége, thought any longer of asking for his intervention. This is proved in a striking manner by the action of the towns of the bishopric of Liége during the fiercest of their contests with bishop Adolph de la Mark. Instead of citing him before Louis of Bavaria, who would not have lost the opportunity of pronouncing in their favour, and, in default of effective assistance, would at least have granted them writs which they could have used to justify their conduct, the towns addressed ineffective appeals to the pope. They disregarded the only authority capable of furnishing them with a legal right to oppose the claims of their bishop. It never occurred to them to use their only opportunity of raising themselves to the rank of free towns. Clearly this was due to the fact that the consciousness of belonging to the empire was gone, and that henceforth the horizon of their political life was bounded by the narrow limits of their bishop's principality.

Instead of a nominal suzerainty like the emperor's, the power exercised in Flanders by the king of France was real and very active. The towns in conflict with Guy of Dampierre did not fail to profit by it. We have seen how they placed themselves under the protection of the crown [1] in order to secure a safeguard against the count. For the moment they were dependent only on the royal jurisdiction and enjoyed a position analogous to that of the free towns of Germany. But the democratic revolution of 1302, which overthrew the patrician *Leliaerts*, also broke the ties which had just been formed between the house of Capet and the communes. These ties were never subsequently re-established. After the definitive peace between Flanders and France, the kings no longer sought the alliance of the towns. Their policy was henceforth to conciliate the count, and in order to attach him to their cause, they lent him their assistance to suppress the rebellions of the towns. It was thanks to the French armies that Louis of Nevers in 1328, and Louis of Mâle in 1380, were able to triumph over the two most formidable urban revolts known in the history of the Low Countries. Thus the weakness of the suzerain in the bishopric of Liége and his power in the county of Flanders had the same result. Both ended by benefitting the prince. The emperor by not using his influence on behalf of the towns, the king by exerting his influence against them after helping them for a time, hindered them from attaining

1. See p. 144.

the political independence at which they aimed. In spite of the heroism displayed by the towns, the princes in the end carried the day.

Further it must not be forgotten that municipal exclusiveness not only forbade the towns to unite in a common effort but also aroused the opposition of all the interests threatened by such narrowness. The nobles and the clergy made common cause with the prince in resisting the encroachments of the burghers. The cause of the towns was at bottom only the cause of a privileged group, whose victory would have meant its overwhelming supremacy and would have been injurious to everyone outside it. The particularism of the towns came into collision with other privileged interests. It was unable to break up the framework of the territorial state, and was forced, whether it pleased or not, to find a place within it.

The towns at least succeeded in winning a paramount place in the organization of the state. If, in the social hierarchy, the third estate yielded precedence to the clergy and the nobility, in all the principalities of the Low Countries, its political power surpassed that of both the other estates. In Flanders, Brabant, Holland and the bishopric of Liége, its influence in the provincial law courts and estates was infinitely greater than that of the other two orders. The privileges granted to the different subdivisions of the Netherlands allowed a preponderating position to the towns. In Brabant, the " Charter of Cortenberg " (1312) set up a council of government in which, by the side of four knights, sat ten representatives of the towns. In the bishopric of Liége, the court of the XXII, established in 1373 to keep a close watch over the officers of the bishop, consisted of four canons, four nobles and fourteen burghers. In the constitution of the county of Flanders, the town became the dominating element. The three great towns of Ghent, Bruges and Ypres arrogated to themselves the right to represent the whole country and, under the name of the three " members " of Flanders, seized, for their own benefit, after the middle of the 14th century, the power which elsewhere belonged to the local estates as a whole.

In truth, strange as it may seem at first sight, it was the growth of the princely power that first gave to the towns a real opportunity of sharing in the government of the counties and duchies in which they were locally situated. From the time when the revenues of their demesne lands no longer sufficed to defray the expenses necessitated by their policy and their administration, the princes found they were bound to call upon their subjects to add to their resources. The towns, being richer than the clergy and the nobility, paid a larger contribution, but they demanded in return for their services concessions which could not be refused. Nevertheless, in coming to the help of their counts and bishops, they were on the whole strengthening a power which was incompatible with municipal self-government. For, from the end of the 13th century, the princes clearly and constantly tended to increase their prerogatives, and to concentrate in their hands as much authority as they could. The lawyers with whom they surrounded themselves, after the example of Philip the Fair, never dreamt of any government which was not despotic in character. They soon taught their princely patrons to follow in the steps of the French kings. In Hainault, Albert of Bavaria tried to introduce a salt tax in 1364 and, under his successor, the lawyer, Philip of Leyden, wrote a manual of statecraft, in which the theory of absolute sovereignty was enunciated without any reservations. In Flanders especially, new institutions sprang up which increased the growing centralization and involved the steady extension of the idea of "lordship." The principle that the prince's will had the force of law became more and more universally accepted.

So long as the different territories of the Low Countries were independent of one another, and had each its own reigning house, the power of the prince nowhere became absolute. But when the house of Burgundy had succeeded in bringing under its control the small feudal states of Flanders and Lorraine, a monarchical policy could develop itself with tenfold vigour owing to its increased resources. Under Philip the Good (1419—1467) the work of unification was completed; the Burgundian state made the greater part of the Netherlands something of a unity, and acquired the centralizing institutions indispensable to the maintenance of such a policy.

II.

THE CONFLICT BETWEEN THE MUNICIPALITIES AND THE MONARCHY IN THE 15TH CENTURY.

While in France and England the modern state found its chief adversaries in the great nobles, in the Low Countries it was the towns that hindered its progress. The more the old system had favoured them, the more desperately they defended it. Force was in the end needed to overcome their resistance.

Nothing could be more mistaken than to see in Philip the Good, as has too often been the case, the mortal foe of the great towns, a tyrant determined upon their ruin and seeking every opportunity to injure them. Philip was fully conscious that his power and position in Europe depended on the riches of the Low Countries. He knew that their prosperity was too intimately bound up with that of the townsfolk for him to think of injuring them. The real truth is that his policy of centralization was incompatible with municipal self-government as understood by the Middle Ages. The sovereignty of the state could not give way before municipal privileges. It was bound to bring the towns under the ordinary law and to sacrifice their particular interests to those of the state as a whole. In combating the prerogatives of the towns, the prince was evidently doing what was best for himself. Yet at the same time he was also acting for the advantage of the great majority of his subjects. He considered his " supremacy " and his " lordship " as the guarantee of "public welfare" and thus justified his claim to obedience. Henceforth the great communes ceased to exist as so many immunities beyond the reach of the central power. The prince shared with them the nomination of their magistrates, audited their accounts by his own officers, prevented them from exploiting the small towns and the peasants, forbade them to fill his dominions with their "foreign burghers," and compelled them, whether they liked it or not, to acquiesce in the right of appeal from the municipal courts to his own supreme tribunal.

It is important to notice that the prince achieved his end without any great difficulty. It is clear that the privileges the towns claimed to uphold against him, had had their day and were doomed to disappear. Everybody, except the burghers themselves, was eager to get rid of municipal immunities, for they had now become an obstacle to the new forces, which, since the beginning of the 15th century, exercised a growing influence upon economic development. The progress of capitalism, of navigation and the means of communication in general, demanded the abolition of the impediments that the policy of the towns threw in the way of freedom. Henceforward commerce on a large scale was brought into conflict with the restrictive economic ideals of the towns, just as the towns themselves had, in their infancy, been confronted by the incompatible manorial economics of feudalism. Foreign trade demanded the abolition of the privileged markets, the staples, and other industrial monopolies. It also required a single code of law binding on the whole state, and therefore the suppression of municipal franchises which had become a hindrance to liberty.

The burghers, who had long enjoyed a privileged position, were naturally bent upon defending it. Instead of adapting themselves to the needs of the time, they remained obstinately devoted to the past. If foreign competition interfered with their export trade, they did not make the slightest effort to win it back by overhauling their methods of manufacture; they saw no hope of safety but in increased protection. In the midst of the changes which were taking place around them, they preserved their unshaken confidence in the mediæval legislation that had created their greatness. They thought that a loss of their outworn privileges would lead inevitably to their " total destruction and destitution." They did not admit that those hopelessly antiquated franchises only constituted so many stumbling blocks to commercial activity. Bruges might see the merchants abandon her for Antwerp; Dordrecht might note the steady growth of the port of Amsterdam; but neither would understand that their privileges, by turning away the stranger from their marts, were the real cause of their decay. Experience taught them nothing, and they remained deaf to the voice of councillors who predicted that, in acting as they were doing, " they would utterly destroy their existing trade."

It is then certain that, in their conflict with the towns, the Burgundian princes were on the whole acting in the interests of the public. They rallied round them not only the clergy, the nobility and the peasants, but also that class of new men, who, in the 15th century, were beginning to develop a system of trade under which capitalism secured the freest expansion. Furthermore, within the towns themselves, a considerable party of the rich burghers pronounced for the princes. In increasing numbers the better class of townsfolk began to abandon commerce and to seek in the service of the state an honourable and lucrative career. Hampered by the exclusive spirit of the crafts and disturbed by the slackening of the industry of the towns, the sons of the patricians thronged into the liberal professions or took up official careers. New institutions created by the centralized monarchy, courts of justice, departments of finance and administrative offices of every kind, drew them away from municipal politics and bound them to the service of the prince who paid them. For the same reason that, during the Burgundian period, the nobility transformed itself by degrees into a nobility of courtiers, the upper class in the towns now provided the prince with an assured supply of recruits for the administrative offices which were continually multiplying owing to the growth of his power.

To counterbalance so many circumstances unfavourable to their cause, it was now imperative that the towns should help one another. But that was just what their exclusive absorption in local and class interests prevented. They failed to combine or to come to an understanding with each other. Jealousy caused them to abandon one another in the hour of peril. In 1437 Bruges found herself deserted by all Flanders in the struggle with Philip the Good. In 1452 Ghent experienced the same fate. With the exception of Ninove, all the towns of the surrounding district abandoned it at the critical moment. In spite of entreaties the other " members " of the county confined themselves to offering the rebels their good offices in reconciling them with the duke. In such a state of affairs it is not astonishing that in the reign of Philip the Good, the traditional conflict between the towns and the state came almost everywhere to an end.

Liége, it is true, fought against the duke of Burgundy with incredible desperation and, as is well known, paid for its heroic obstinacy against Charles the Bold by its utter destruction. But Liége was not a Burgundian town. It was not fighting solely for its franchises, but for its independence in secular matters of the ecclesiastical principality of which it was the capital, and it had on its side the whole population of the bishopric. Liége saw in the house of Burgundy a conqueror and a foreigner, even more than an enemy of municipal privilege. Above all it must not be forgotten that the interference of the French king explains both the boldness of the town and the harshness with which it was treated by its conqueror.

In no part of their own lands did the dukes of Burgundy act with the cruelty shewn towards Liége. Moreover it was only in Flanders, that is to say in the country where the towns enjoyed the most extensive privileges and had also encroached most boldly on the prerogatives of the prince, that the Burgundian dukes had to take arms against the burghers. The rising at Bruges in 1436—1437 was not indeed very formidable. But Ghent did not hesitate to confront its sovereign with that remarkable dourness and tenacity of which its history furnishes so many examples. Thanks to the number of its " foreign burghers," to the peasants whom it enrolled by force and to the English mercenaries whom it hired, the powerful commune was able to hold the blockading forces in check for more than a year. But, in spite of all their courage, its militia could no longer meet a regular army in a pitched battle. The progress of the art of war gave to these craftsmen turned soldiers no chance of victory. The bloody defeat they suffered at Gavere, on July 23rd, 1453, at the hands of Philip's Picard and Burgundian veterans, shewed in unmistakable fashion the hopeless weakness of the military system of the communes.

Ghent did not, as after Roosebeke, attempt to continue a hopeless resistance. On July 30th two thousand of her burghers came and knelt in their shirts before duke Philip and begged for mercy. They undertook to pay an indemnity of 350,000 gold *ridders* and, in token of submission, to wall up one of the town gates and to keep another shut every Thursday. This atonement to the prince's offended majesty was, moreover, only the least part of the punishment. Ghent, like Bruges in 1437, had to renounce its almost absolute independence and the supremacy over its neighbours which it had till then enjoyed. All customs contrary to the letter of its charters were abolished. The deans of the three " members," the crafts, the *poorters* and the weavers, ceased to have any voice in the election of magistrates; the count's steward recovered control over the administration of the town; the privileges of the " foreign burghers " were curtailed; the *échevins* lost all right to call before them a law suit in which a burgher was involved, if he were willing to accept a jurisdiction other than that of the commune; and finally and above all, the small towns and the villages of the *châtellenie* were withdrawn from the power of Ghent. Thus Ghent was in its turn brought under the ordinary law. Robbed of its lordship and of the franchises which it had added in such numbers to its legal privileges, it was now simply just like any other town and was reduced to the level of its fellows. Still, it was only the political privileges which were abolished by the duke; he did not deprive Ghent of its right to the staple, nor did he interfere with its municipal self-government. He even helped it to repair the misfortunes of the war by granting it, only a few weeks after the battle of Gavere, the right to hold two fairs.

This circumstance may be regarded as quite characteristic of the duke's policy towards the towns. Philip
made no attempt to impose an arbitrary government
upon them. He allowed the local government, which
had grown up in the towns, to remain. He respected
the liberties granted by his predecessors. Above all
he avoided arousing discontent by any untimely or
meddlesome interference. He took care to choose
from nobles or officials, acquainted with local manners
and customs, the "commissioners," who represented
him when the yearly appointment of the magistrates
was made, and their accounts audited. In most
respects, moreover, the intervention of his commissioners was distinctly beneficial. After examining the
recommendations made by them, and entered in the
communal registers, it is impossible not to appreciate
the conscientiousness with which they nearly all set
themselves to accomplish their task. Many useless
expenses were suppressed, many abuses abolished;
and many beneficial reforms were brought about by
them in the municipal finances.

The Burgundian government tried hard to discover
remedies for the economic decay due, in most of the
towns of Flanders, to the dwindling of the cloth
industry. In the interests of the towns the importation of cloth and yarn from England was forbidden.
The efforts of Bruges to prevent the silting up of the
Zwyn were encouraged. Everything possible was
done to help the development of the Antwerp fairs.
The towns of Holland were assisted in their conflict
with the Hansa, and thanks to this they succeeded in
appropriating the carrying trade of their opponents.
In the crisis, brought about by alterations in the course

of trade, which had left Bruges on one side, and by English competition, which was ruining the Flemish cloth industry, the state spared no effort to help the distressed communes. But clearly it could not save them in spite of themselves. The narrowness of municipal policy often dictated to the central authority measures which it would certainly never have taken if left to itself. Pulled in different directions by towns whose interests were incompatible, the state did not always see the path clear before it; it hesitated, felt its way, and often made contradictory decisions. We find the duke maintaining Bruges in her staple rights, and at the same time encouraging the growth of the Antwerp fairs, which were ruining the old commercial monopolies. In Flanders, to satisfy Ypres, he repressed the rural cloth manufacture in the neighbourhood of that town, though elsewhere he authorized and protected it. We see from this hesitating policy, that, influenced alike by the tendencies of the past and those of the future, he was unable to take up a clear line of his own. He attempted the impossible feat of reconciling the new capitalism " which always seeks liberty " with the old municipal protection. The one end that the Burgundian policy was resolutely bent upon accomplishing was the subordination of the towns to the superior power of the prince, that is, to the state.

The new official system of centralization also provided a considerable number of towns with fresh resources and contributed to reconcile them to the new administration which had been imposed upon them. The establishment of a university at Louvain in 1426, of supreme courts of justice at Ghent, Brussels and Mechlin, of financial chambers at Lille, Brussels

N

and the Hague, caused the establishment in those places of numerous officials, lawyers, and subordinate employees of all kinds. Students, suitors, and officials of the revenue departments flocked to the same towns. Both the new residents and the new floating population were a constant source of abundant profit to the inhabitants. Thus the civil administration contributed in its turn to the maintenance of the life of the towns by the creation of great institutions involving a large resident population engaged in serving them, such as the ecclesiastical authorities had alone possessed up to that time. These processes kept up town life, but changed its character. The residence of a large body of officers of the state in the very midst of the burghers necessarily diminished municipal exclusiveness. When they were always in touch with the general organization of the country, the towns could no longer regard themselves as little worlds apart. They felt that they were elements of a larger whole and that, instead of initiating policy, they were bound to follow where they were led. However suspicious of the state the small burghers were, they put up with it because they feared it and even profited by it. As for the wealthy classes, we have already said that they made haste to benefit by their opportunities, and to transfer to the service of the state an activity which till then had only been exercised within the narrow limits of municipal politics.

It is true that these changes were not carried through without resistance. After the death of Philip the Good (1467), the haughty absolutism of Charles the Bold seriously threatened the results already attained. When Charles was still only count of Charolais, he one day boasted before the people of Brussels that "by St. George, if he ever became their duke, he would let them know it and they should not act towards him as they had towards his father, who had been too easy with them, had enriched them, and made them the proud men they were."

Charles kept his word precisely. The sack of Liége taught the towns that they now had a pitiless master, "who preferred their hatred to their contempt." The prince overrode at his pleasure the municipal self-government that Philip had respected. Ancient customs, established rights and deep-rooted privileges were trampled under foot. At Ghent, the election of *échevins* was handed over entirely to the duke's commissioners; the three " members " into which the townsmen were divided, were abolished; for the future the whole of the inhabitants were to form, at his will, "only one body and community." In Holland, Charles claimed for himself the nomination of the municipal magistrates. His arbitrary and levelling radicalism thought for a moment of substituting at Liége the scientific rigour of Roman law for the old local customs. A despot by nature he was still more so by conviction. He sincerely believed that the absolute power of the sovereign was the sole guarantee of order and of that stern and equal justice, which he claimed to have enthroned in his dominions. But his internal government met with the same fate as his foreign policy. His pride and unreasonable obstinacy ruined both alike. The catastrophe which befel Charles before the walls of Nancy (1477), gave the signal for a particularist reaction that all but destroyed the state created by Philip the Good.

The more rigorously the despotism of the dukes had justified by the common law its intolerable encroachments, the more the towns sought to regain their privileges. All the great communes hastened to profit by the annihilation of the ducal army and the disorder of their young princess's[1] affairs to re-establish their franchises and to revive their ancient methods of government. Everywhere the crafts took up arms, and democratic government was set up again, just as it had existed in the 14th century. But its success lasted only a moment. Hardly was it restored when its powerlessness was apparent. The old spirit of municipal particularism soon let loose once more the old spirit of universal rivalry. The country districts and the small towns, falling once more under the yoke of the great communes, declared against them. Bruges and Ghent excited the ill-will of Antwerp, whose development was threatened by their policy of protection. Accordingly Antwerp at once went back to the side of the prince. The towns of Holland, which in great measure owed their growing maritime supremacy to Burgundian policy, also abandoned their opposition after the first moment of excitement. Flanders alone refused to lay down her arms. The stronger and more privileged the towns of Flanders had been in times past, the less capable they were of understanding the necessity for reconciling their interests with those of the state.

The crafts of the Flemish towns perceived that their forces were not strong enough to give them the victory. Recalling the action of the *Leliaerts* in 1302,

---

1. Charles left as his heir his only child, Mary of Burgundy, then aged twenty.

they turned to the king of France. They summoned Louis XI. to their rescue, just as their ancient enemies appealed to Philip the Fair for aid against the crafts. The democracy sought the same support as the decaying patriciate, the help of the foreigner. French mercenaries arrived to do the fighting on its behalf, for the communal militia confined itself to keeping watch on the ramparts and did not venture to meet regular troops in the open field. The war was clumsily conducted by Maximilian of Austria, who had married Mary of Burgundy in August 1477; accordingly it dragged on for a long time with vicissitudes on which we need not now dwell. The obstinacy of Ghent prolonged hostilities until 1492, even after all chance of success had vanished. Maximilian was a foreigner, and he showed a lack of intelligence in parading an absolutism modelled on that of Charles the Bold. He quarrelled with a large number of the nobles after the death of Mary; his resources were scanty; he was frequently absent in Germany, where he had been elected king of the Romans in 1486. These circumstances sufficiently explain the length of the resistance offered by Ghent, notwithstanding the fact that France was a long way off and supported the townsmen with no great energy. In reality outside Flanders, and even in Flanders outside Ghent, the partisans of the old municipal policy and of the urban democracy by which it was supported, were only a feeble minority. Ghent herself gradually abandoned its principles. Under the domination of the demagogue John of Coppenhole, formerly clerk to the *échevins,* who had risen to power during the troubles, the burgesses lived in a state of anarchy and violence against which, ultimately, a large part of the burghers rose in revolt. The craft of the boatmen, the most influential of the trade guilds since the decline of the cloth trade had robbed the weavers of all their influence, demanded the end of a ruinous and aimless war. To secure his position, Coppenhole had their leader beheaded and pitted against them the lesser crafts, whose extreme industrial particularism was the mainstay of extreme municipal particularism. A shoemaker became captain-general of the commune. But the boatmen rebelled, and Coppenhole in his turn mounted the scaffold. After that, peace was only a question of days. It was concluded at Cadzand on July 29th 1492, and brought Ghent back to the state of things set up within its walls after the peace of Gavere.

With the capitulation of the most indomitable of the towns, the period of municipal wars in the Low Countries came to an end. The accession of Philip the Handsome, the son of Mary of Burgundy and Maximilian, in 1494, gave power to a national prince, and soothed public feeling. Thus the triumph of the state put an end to the conflict which had raged for more than a century between the state and the communes, the state standing for the modern principle of centralized monarchy and the communes for the mediæval principle of particularist autonomy. But that triumph did not crush the towns beneath an absolute government. They still had strength enough, if not to contend with the state, yet at any rate to exercise a great influence in its affairs, and to insist upon due regard for their interests and wishes.

CHAPTER IX.

THE TOWNS DURING THE RENAISSANCE.

I. The Economic Revolution and its Influence on the Government of the Towns.—II. The Population of the Towns during the 16th Century.—III. The Rising at Ghent against Charles V.

I.

The Economic Revolution and its Influence on the Government of the Towns.

Since the beginning of the Burgundian period, political, economic and social changes had little by little modified the position of the Netherlandish towns, had radically altered their commerce and manufactures and changed the nature of their population. These changes not only provoked the struggle with the prince but also decided its issue. They were so rapidly and clearly marked in the first years of the 16th century that, after the reign of Philip the Handsome, the burghers found themselves face to face with a state of affairs completely different from every point of view from that which had, during four centuries, determined their interests, aims and institutions. To begin with, from the political point of view the sovereign had, by alliances and by good fortune in marriage treaties, gained a power that rendered him the mightiest ruler in Europe, against whom it was impossible to rebel.

Charles V, the son and successor of Philip the Handsome, became master of Spain, Milan, the kingdom of
Naples, the domains of the house of Austria, and
the empire; he aspired to universal dominion, and the
provinces of his Netherlandish patrimony, administered in his name by governors (Margaret of Austria
and then Mary of Burgundy), were obedient to his
orders, being only too pleased with the internal self-
government which he allowed them to enjoy. Charles
cleverly avoided ruffling the old national traditions or,
by a crushing absolutism, sowing a discontent that
could not failed to be turned to advantage by his rival,
the king of France. Furthermore, in spite of their
small area, the Low Countries possessed such wealth
that the emperor's credit was in a large measure
dependent upon them. It was important, then, for
him to humour them.

Indeed the peace enjoyed by the Netherlands, under
Philip the Handsome, after the civil broils of Maximilian's reign, had not only restored prosperity but had
carried it to a point never reached before. The admirable
position of the country, which, in the Middle Ages,
had made it the centre of the commerce of the north,
gave it, in the world widened by the discoveries of the
Spaniards and the Portuguese, a correspondingly
widened economic importance. From the beginning
of the 16th century, Antwerp became the warehouse
of the world's carrying trade. The influence that it
acquired, between about 1520 and 1580, has never
belonged to any town before or since. Never has any
port possessed such an exclusive supremacy, exercised
so strong an attraction and displayed such a cosmopolitan character. It presented a unique spectacle during

those years of astonishing progress when, by extraordinary good fortune, it was at once the greatest
market and the greatest banking centre of the world.
Ships and capital were drawn to the town; all lan-
guages could be heard there. By her beauty as well
as by her wealth, Antwerp deserved to be called one of
the flowers of the world; her prosperity made the Low
Countries "a land common to all nations." As a
necessary result of her pre-eminence, all the surrounding provinces followed the lead of Antwerp; she
communicated to them her activity, permeated them
with her spirit and hastened the transition from the
economic methods of the Middle Ages to those of
modern times.

The most striking feature of the modern system is, as
is generally recognized, the preponderance of capital.
The rise of a capitalist class was encouraged all over
Europe by the development of strong monarchies,
based upon centralized institutions, by the growing
financial needs of the chief states, which kept pace
with the increasing frequency of war, and by the
general spread of the machinery and instruments
of credit, by geographical discoveries, by the advance
of science, by the growth of a spirit of enterprise and,
finally, by the moral upheaval of the Renaissance. All
these conditions favoured the growth of a class of bold
adventurers, great merchants, bankers and speculators,
as keenly devoted to the search for wealth as was the
humanist to the knowledge of the wisdom of antiquity,
and as devoid of scruple as a diplomatist trained in
the school of Machiavelli. As a result of their
activity, economic history developed on the same
lines as the history of art. The contrast between the

new capitalists and the patricians of the Middle Ages
is as striking as that between Fra Angelico and
Raphael, or between Van Eyck and Frans Floris.
The capital they controlled was infinitely greater than
that of the ancient *poorters,* and they dealt in a market
of infinitely greater extent. Again, they did not
spring from the ranks of the old burgher merchants.
These merchants, when they felt the effect of the
economic revolution, were either ruined or changed by
degrees into a class of men of private means, or they
became officials or lawyers. The " new men " of the
Renaissance were in fact adventurers. They had no
ancestors, no family traditions, and their fierce
eagerness to acquire riches manifested itself with that
peculiar intensity and vigour which characterize all
the new forces set free at that passionate period.

From every quarter men of this stamp were drawn
towards Antwerp by a natural impulse, as the *con-
quistadors* of their time were drawn to the New World.
They hurried from Germany, Italy, Spain and the
provinces of the Low Countries, to try their fortunes
as brokers, banking agents, exporters, commission
agents or speculators. The more fortunate soon
accumulated immense wealth, while others were overwhelmed by crashing failures. They lived a feverish life,
subject to all the chance ups and downs caused by war,
by the cornering of goods and the fluctuations of the
money market. In proportion as economic life in the
Middle Ages had been regulated, supervised, sheltered
from free competition and partitioned into local
compartments and professional groups which were
protected against one another, in that degree it now
expanded, contemning the old barriers and honoured

usages, unfettered, unscrupulous and pitiless. The liberal and capitalist character that it gave to the commerce of Antwerp necessarily spread abroad, and we sóon find the industry of the Low Countries modified by its influence.

From the beginning of the 16th century, the market of Antwerp absorbed the greater part of the produce of the Low Countries. Antwerp gave the orders, and became more and more the source of the prosperity of the whole country. Bruges, still faithful to her obsolete legal rights, protested in vain against the flagrant violation of her staple privileges. Her port was deserted. The more she clamoured to attract merchants, the more they gave her a wide berth and turned towards her younger rival, where the principle of commercial liberty had gained the victory over privilege and monopoly. The town crafts in their turn vainly endeavoured to struggle against a position before which they were as powerless as the communal levies had been before regular armies. Their decadence grew more marked from year to year. The towns of Flanders and Brabant had in vain persuaded the dukes of Burgundy to prohibit the importation of English stuffs, the cheapness of which gave them admittance despite all efforts. Thousands of pieces of English kerseys were unloaded on the quays of Antwerp every year, though ruin was falling on the cloth trade of the Netherlands. In 1545 at Ypres "the business of the drapery trade was so fallen off and diminished" that only about a hundred looms were still working. At Ghent in 1543 the looms numbered no more than twenty-five. The same state of things was to be found in Brabant. At Brussels in 1537 there were no blue dyers left. The promise of a subsidy of 600 florins was needed to draw one of them to the town.

This decline was fatal. To maintain itself in the face of a strenuous competition, encouraged by the commercial interests of Antwerp, the ancient cloth manufacture in the Netherlandish towns would have had to renounce entirely its old-fashioned organization, abandon the processes which the practice of centuries had made habitual, and sacrifice to industrial necessities its traditional claim to absolute protection and all the other consequences of a legal position made for a dead epoch. But how could the artisans be expected to break with methods which to them seemed bound up with their existence? Could they get beyond the narrow horizon which had limited their view for so many centuries? There could be no doubt as to their answer. In fact, the government of the crafts could only have been overturned by a violent revolution, by a complete rearrangement of the whole system of municipal government. This was too old, too deeply rooted in tradition and use to make its modification possible. Accordingly the mediæval municipal system went on vegetating and collapsed in slow decay. All the measures taken to help it failed.

In contrast with the drapery trade in the towns, the cloth manufacture in the country districts entered upon a career of astonishing progress. Reduced, during the whole of the Middle Ages, to a precarious and miserable existence by the jealously guarded privileges of the towns, it had begun to expand here and there during the Burgundian period, in spite of many difficulties and constant complaints. Then suddenly, towards the end of the first third of the 16th century, it became very prosperous. The result was the growth of a new system of industry, fundamentally different from the old corporate organization, which still existed side by side with it, and as well adapted to the new economic order as the guild system was incompatible with it. Free from all the fetters with which municipal regulation had narrowly confined the artisan, the new development answered all the requirements of capitalist enterprise. Under the new conditions there were no limits to the output, no crafts uniting the artisans against the employer, interfering with the rate of wages, fixing the conditions of apprenticeship and limiting the hours of work. Above all there were no privileges restricting admission to the trade to burghers only, and excluding "foreigners," as all new burghers had long been styled. Here every man was sure of being employed, provided he was able-bodied and knew how to throw a shuttle. No one troubled about his past or where he came from, while the man himself, treating with his employer as an isolated individual, perforce submitted to the terms imposed upon him by the master, since he was only too thankful to have found a means of earning his bread. Thus in the villages round Ypres, in the castelry of Bailleul, at Bergues-Saint-Winnoc, in the neighbourhood of Lille, but above all at Hondschoote and Armentières, there arose a real industrial proletariate. Miserable wretches and vagabonds drifted there from all parts of the country. More than that, the evil plight of industry in the towns drove the work-people of the great communes into the open country and caused the strange sight of an exodus from the towns into the villages. In short, in order to compete with English cloth, the Low Countries had to undergo a transformation similar to that which had taken place in England itself. The contrast between the young industrial communities of the 16th century, and the old towns, recalls a like contrast between privileged boroughs, like Worcester and Evesham, and the manufacturing towns of Manchester, Sheffield and Birmingham, which then begin for the first time to claim a place for themselves in history.

Naturally the " new cloth trade " worked for the Antwerp market; from there came the orders to complete hundreds or even thousands of pieces for a single merchant. Moreover the same thing happened in the case of many other industries which were called into existence in the same way by capitalism and economic freedom. A great development of the iron industry and of coal-mining in the provinces of Liége, Namur and Hainault, went on independently of the town crafts, under the conditions of the common law, and directed by individual enterprise. There too the industrial proletariate first appeared in the country districts.

This social system spread immediately to the towns. If the crafts kept a jealous eye on the old industries and thereby doomed them to stagnation, they could not hinder the introduction of manufactures unknown to the Middle Ages, or subject them to their regulations. The capitalists did not neglect the opportunity of profiting from these circumstances. During the first half of the 16th century, the weaving of satin and baize and of twilled material, the making of ribbons and glass-blowing, were introduced in several ancient municipalities. Thus the new organization made its way into the towns alongside the privileged corporations. At Valenciennes, for example, the manufacture of serges was started by wealthy capitalist employers. Most of the workmen employed by the trade came from the neighbouring villages, whither they returned on Saturday evening, to pass the Sunday with their families and to take home the scanty wage which they had earned by working in the town all the week. Carpet-making and the linen industry also show us the crafts retreating before the invading force of capital. In spite of the outcries of the town artisans, free labour, that is to say country labour, was almost exclusively employed. Carpet-making occupied thousands of weavers throughout Flanders. The linen industry was carried on with vigour in a great number of parishes round Oudenarde. The little family workshops, in groups of thirty to sixty under the direction of *winkelmeesters* (workshop masters), were at the disposal of the employers in the towns. Every Sunday the work done during the week was taken to them and exchanged for the raw material to be worked up during the following week.

II.

THE POPULATION OF THE TOWNS IN THE 16TH CENTURY.

It was necessary to describe in some detail the economic movements of the 16th century in order to make intelligible the changes through which the burgher class passed at that period. We have said enough on

that subject to show how different was the position of
the privileged municipalities henceforward from what
it had been in the Middle Ages. They had lost the
monopoly of industry. The progress of capitalism, as
well as progress in methods of manufacture, had made
it impossible for them to maintain unchanged a
system of regulations which only suited the needs of
a period that had passed away. It is true that this
system had not entirely perished. The policy of
protection for the burgher tradesmen still governed
all that had to do with the food supply in the local
market. The crafts busied with the feeding of the
population still held their privileged place. Butchers,
bakers, smiths, joiners, shoemakers, etc., continued to
possess the sole rights of supplying the daily needs
of the burghers. Driven out of the great industries
by the country workmen, the crafts were all the more
eager to retain their remaining sphere of operations.
With that end in view their regulations multiplied
and constantly increased in minuteness. The corporations jealously shared out among each other
the narrow area that was still under their control.
Each craft spied upon its neighbours, and the least
transgression of the rights of one of them was the
signal for interminable law suits. Between the turners
and the joiners, the coopers and the carpenters, the
leather workers and the harness makers, in short,
between all the groups of artisans who lived on the
local market, litigation was incessant. At the same
time every craft withdrew into its shell and became
less and less accessible to new-comers. The rank of
master workman tended to become hereditary, and
simple journeymen could seldom attain it, placed as it

was beyond their reach by the exorbitant fines which had to be paid before it could be gained.

Little by little the craft guilds of each district became divided into two distinct groups : an upper group, which was practically a civic aristocracy, making plentiful and easy profits under the shelter of protection; the lower, a class of domestic workers, sharing the work of their masters, well treated by them as a rule, but deprived of any hope of ever improving their condition. The social aspect of the guilds, entering upon a new phase, lost all the vigour and energy it had shown in the Middle Ages. The masters, attending only to their own interests, tried to evade the expenses entailed by keeping up the corporate life of these societies. It was often necessary for the state to interfere and compel them to accept the office of *reward* or *vinder*. Most of the crafts were in debt; their ancient charities were maintained with difficulty. On the other hand their political privileges were useless except to the masters. The masters monopolized the representation of the craft guilds in all their dealings with the municipal authorities. To use an expression as exact as it is undignified, we may say that they only used their privileges in the spirit of hucksters.

In opposition to these ancient bodies, petrified in privilege, the workers in the new industries in the towns affected by the action of capitalism, began to show a constantly increasing activity, and an energy which kept pace with the progress of the export trade. Between their position and that of the crafts we find once more, but in a very different form, the contrast already noticed in the Middle Ages between the

o

artisans engaged in the cloth manufacture and those occupied in other callings. Mere wage-earners, like the fullers and weavers of former times, these workmen enjoyed no rights of corporate life such as their predecessors had possessed. They were exposed without redress to the exploitation of their employers. The state and the municipality, so careful of the smaller trades, abandoned them to their fate. If the public authority interfered on their behalf, it was only with the object of reorganizing their charities. This circumstance in itself throws a strong light on the miserable condition to which they were reduced. A large number of the craftsmen were only beggars working under compulsion, or the children of beggars, whom the funds of the new charitable societies had apprenticed to some craft. Others, as we have seen above, came from the country to hire out their labour in the town, and did not share in any sense in its corporate rights. They formed a floating element in the population, wandering hither and thither as prosperity waxed or waned. Strangers passing through the country were astonished to find in most of the towns wealthy merchants living side by side with a poor and discontented populace.

The discontent was unavailing and fruitless. An unorganized proletariate was incapable of drilling its forces to take common action. It had not sufficient consciousness of its common interests to form a distinct class. It was as completely outside the social life of the town as it was outside the protection of its law. It had absolutely no share in its municipal activity. As conservative politically as they were economically, the towns carefully excluded this class from any share in the municipal franchise. The qualifications of burgesses remained in the 16th century exactly what they had been in the 14th. The " members " of the municipal corporation had not undergone the least alteration, though all had changed around them. At Ghent, for instance, in spite of the decay of the cloth trade, the weavers' guild preserved its ancient preponderating authority in the general meetings of the commune. The place given to the different crafts in the administration of the town was measured by their past, not by their present, importance. Whether a branch of industry languished or prospered, the corporations representing it continued permanently to enjoy the rights which had been won by them, and which were sanctioned by their privileges. Thus the representation of interests, which the democratic government had been at such pains to establish in the towns, became now nothing but a caricature. It was too stereotyped to answer any longer to the needs of the age. Established institutions remained unchanged; no one troubled to find out whether they still corresponded with the facts of the case and had their appropriate share of rights and duties. In fact the municipal organization, by simply remaining what the " commons " had made it in the 14th century, had become by force of circumstances purely aristocratic. The course of economic and social evolution had resulted in the control of the town being left entirely in the hands of a small number of privileged groups. Burgher rights, which formerly had been extended to the whole population of the towns, were now confined to a small section of it. This limited body constituted a caste, almost closed to the large working class which had been called into existence by the new capitalism. Already the logic of facts was defining the meaning of the word *bourgeois* in the narrow and exclusive sense in which it is still used by the modern socialist.

Thus the industrial proletariate was carefully excluded from all legal right to take part in the public affairs of the town. The men composing it, moreover, lived under such different conditions, and were for the most part so wretched that they never so much as thought of claiming political rights for themselves. Yet it is none the less true that the lower classes more than once rose in serious revolts, and caused the authorities lively disquiet. But these disturbances were always due to sheer misery. The considerable increase of prices, which occurred all over Europe during the 16th century, and made itself felt in the Low Countries from about 1550, aggravated the wretchedness of the condition of the people, because the slight rise in wages only partly compensated for the fall in the value of money. We are, therefore, not astonished to observe from that time onwards numerous risings, brought about perhaps by the imposition of a new tax, or more often by the rise in the price of corn or beer. These riots, however, though sometimes violent, were always of very short duration, and only resulted in the pillage of granaries or the looting of the houses of some of the merchants. Unlike the men of the mediæval communes, the famished crowd of men, women and children who were driven into insurrection, were without arms, and the municipal militia easily got the better of them. A few executions for the sake of example served to put a stop to the trouble. The magistrates reduced the price of bread for a short time, and order was restored until a new crisis in their misery provoked a new outburst of impotent fury.

III.

THE RISING AT GHENT AGAINST CHARLES V.

At last it happened that the crafts, discontented with the central power, appealed to the very proletariate which they had so habitually and carefully disregarded. Such was the case, for example, in 1539, after the conflict between the governor, Mary of Hungary, and the people of Ghent, when the town refused the aid required to withstand an invasion of the Low Countries by Francis I. The " members " of the artisan guilds profited by the opportunity to re-establish the municipal government abolished by the peace of Gavere,[1] that is to say, to return to the direct government of the commune by its three " members " and to all the particularism of the Middle Ages. It is impossible to doubt the spirit that animated them, when we find them, in their hatred of capitalism and economic liberty, demanding the revival of the privilege which forbade the exercise of any manufacture within a radius of three leagues round the town. But almost at once they found themselves swamped by the unprivileged masses. The authority of the deans of the guilds was openly set at nought. Bands of vagabonds poured into the town from the country, filled it with their loud

1. See p. 192.

demands, spread terror by their violence and prepared to sack the monasteries and the houses of the rich. Soon, at Oudenarde, Courtrai, Ypres, Lille, Grammont, Armentières, "the poor folk and others of mean estate" adopted a menacing attitude. But the danger was more apparent than real. The people, left to themselves, fell into anarchy. The turbulence of the crowd was equalled by its military weakness and its political blindness. To resist the forces of the emperor, the rebels dragged to their dilapidated walls the antiquated bombards of the Middle Ages. They also begged for the support of Francis I. But the French king, then at peace with Charles V, hastened to inform the emperor of their strange overtures.

Exasperated by the presumption of the insurgents Charles resolved to inflict exemplary punishment upon Ghent. He came to the place with an imposing military force on February 14th, 1540; he instructed the public prosecutor of the High Court at Mechlin to draw up an indictment against the town. To bring into relief his sovereign power, he took care not to treat Ghent as a belligerent : he professed to see in it merely a rebel. Sentence was pronounced on April 29th. The people of Ghent were proclaimed guilty of sedition and treason. They were in consequence deprived of all their privileges, and were compelled to surrender to their prince the charters guaranteeing them their franchises. All the property belonging to the commune and the crafts, all the arms and the artillery belonging to the town were confiscated. It was decided that "Roland," the big bell of the belfry, should be taken down. The *échevins*, thirty burghers, the dean of the weavers, ten men of each craft, fifty

of the weavers' " member " and fifty *creesers*,[1] bare-
footed, bare-headed and in their shirts, were to sue for
the forgiveness of the emperor. The moat round the
town walls was to be filled up from the Antwerp Gate
to the Scheldt. Moreover the town was to pay its
share of the aid that had been refused, and in addition
a fine of 150,000 gold " Charles." Finally, it was to
repay all those who had been compelled to make it
advances during the disturbances.

The next day, April 30th, the proclamation was
made of the " Caroline Concession," which abolished
for ever the ancient constitution of Ghent and was
destined to remain in force until the fall of the *ancien
régime*. Not only did it make the *échevins* of Ghent
the nominees of the prince, but it suppressed the three
" members " of the corporation and willed that the
whole population should thenceforth form only " one
body and community." The *collace*, that is to say
the great council of the commune, was abolished : it
was replaced by the meeting of certain deputies from
the parishes, chosen by the prince's steward and the
echevins. In this assembly resolutions were decided
by a bare majority of votes. The crafts were reduced
to the position of simple industrial societies, strictly
controlled by the police and the magistrates. The
deans of the guilds were replaced by the *oversten*,
appointed by the steward and the *échevins* ; their classification was completely remodelled and brought into
harmony with the transformed economic situation ; a
number of guilds, no longer answering to any need,
were abolished ; their number fell from fifty-three to
twenty one. Outside its immediate vicinity, the town

1. " Brawlers " ; the name given to those who had administered
the town during the troubles.

lost the remnants of the power it had exercised over
the castelry and also the right of creating foreign
burghers. Finally, to secure its obedience for the
future, a strong fortress was built on the site of the old
monastery of St. Bavon, at the junction of the Scheldt
and the Lys. The new citadel was begun while the
population was still kept in terror by daily executions,
and the halls and plate of the crafts were being sold
by auction.

The severity with which Charles V. treated the town
of Ghent, in which he had been born and towards
which he had till then shown particular goodwill, is
not entirely explained by his firm determination to
demonstrate to the burghers of the Low Countries the
reality of his sovereign power. The Caroline Concession is not merely an act of vengeance from an
angry potentate; it is rather the programme of a
new method of government. It must be regarded as
a long-considered measure, expressing the modern
attitude of the state in dealing with the great communes. It had a twofold aim. The more important
was to subordinate the exclusiveness of the towns and
the protectionist policy of the craft guilds to economic
liberty and capitalist commerce. A contemporary
remarks that " the merchants, who always want
freedom for their trade, were unwilling to visit,
frequent or dwell in Ghent," because of the excessive
franchises of its burghers. Henceforth they came to
settle there in great numbers and founded powerful
houses. Industry, freed from the tutelage of the
privileged corporations, grew rapidly. The town
became the great market for Flemish linen, and when
the canal to Terneuzen, begun in 1547, had given an

opening to the sea, Ghent experienced a new era of
prosperity which went on increasing till the troubled
reign of Philip II, and finally even caused serious
anxiety in Antwerp. In 1565 Guicciardini compared
her to Milan, the richest Italian city of his time. She
had ceased to be a mediæval commune and had
become a modern town.

But if the " Caroline Concession " is the outcome of
a stage in economic development, the motives which
inspired its author were purely political. Charles V.
only reduced the town to such strict subjection in
order to make it incapable of resisting his future
projects. In spite of the modifications made by the
Burgundian government, the constitution of Ghent
still preserved numerous traces of its former democratic character. The *échevins* could not by themselves bind the town. All important questions, and
particularly all financial questions, had to be submitted
to the "three members " of the community. Without
their consent no new tax could be raised, and this
consent was often very difficult to secure, each " member " maintaining that decisions were only valid
when they were unanimous. It was therefore possible
for a single " member " to prevent the imposition of
a tax approved by the rest of the population. Now
since the beginning of the 16th century, the growing
expenses of the prince and especially his continual
wars compelled him to have continual recourse to
subsidies from the States General. We can, therefore,
understand the impatience with which he bore the
pretention of a few craft guilds to upset his plans by
refusing the supplies which he judged indispensable
to carry out his policy. In reality the complicated

machinery of the States General did not allow them to vote at all. The representatives of the different provinces who had seats, "were only charged to listen," and were obliged to consult their constituencies before they were authorised to make any answer. Almost always the resistance of a single town encouraged the others to follow its example. It thus happened that the obstinacy of a single "member," that is to say of a weak minority of the smaller burghers, compromised altogether the grant of a new tax.

To get out of the difficulty thus occasioned, both the governors and the emperor himself had tried to substitute a majority vote for the unanimous vote in the town council. The right of a single voice to veto any proposition was utterly incompatible with the normal working of any kind of government by discussion. Yet the crafts had always insisted upon its being upheld as one of their most precious privileges. Under the circumstances then, we are not surprised to find Charles V. profiting by the revolt of Ghent to suppress a state of things so unfavourable to his interests and to the financial administration of the state. The suppression of the "members" of Ghent gave him a radical solution of his troubles. Henceforth the *échevins* and the notables were only summoned to give their consent to taxation, and that consent was assured beforehand, because the *échevins* were nominated by the agents of the sovereign and the notables always belonged to ancient burgher families which were devoted to his service.

Thus this judgment of 1540 secured the incorporation of the town in the state and showed clearly the

tendency of the monarch's policy. Unable to deprive
his dominions in the Low Countries of their right to
vote taxes without exciting a general revolt, the
emperor turned the position which he could not take
by assault. By the new constitution thus bestowed
upon Ghent, he sapped the strength of the first town
of Flanders, and Ghent usually gave the lead to the
other towns of the whole county. It is evident that
the " Caroline Concession " laid down the form of
government that he would have been glad to establish
everywhere. But it is also characteristic that he made
no effort to enforce its provisions in the other towns
of Flanders. In spite of the inconveniences to the
central power resulting from their franchises, the
towns against which no grievance could be alleged
preserved their old institutions. The " nations " of
the communes of Brabant in particular, still caused
the governors much anxiety. The government
attained its end by "Acts of Comprehension." [1] The
remembrance of the punishment which Ghent had
suffered made the towns accept them lest worse should
befall. The autocratic tendency was not strong
enough to gain a complete ascendancy. It only
destroyed privileges when it was in a position to
invoke in its favour the terrible law of treason. But
no one had any doubt about the aim of the administration. The franchises that it suffered to continue so
as not to violate tradition, were no longer a serious
obstacle to progress, for everyone knew that any
attempt to make them effective would be the signal
for their abolition.

1. The name given to a decision of the state declaring that an
impost voted by the majority was regarded as accepted also by the
minority.

CHAPTER X.

THE TOWNS DURING THE PERIOD OF THE REFORMATION.

I. SOCIAL AND POLITICAL MOVEMENTS RESULTING FROM THE REFORMATION.—II. THE TOWNS UNDER CALVINIST GOVERNMENT.

I.

SOCIAL AND POLITICAL MOVEMENTS RESULTING FROM THE REFORMATION.

The municipal and economic system of the Middle Ages was already disappearing under the influence of the Renaissance when the Reformation provoked fresh disturbances in the remodelled towns of the Netherlands.

From 1518 the first signs of Lutheranism can be discerned among the cosmopolitan population of Antwerp, and after that time heresy quickly spread from place to place in spite of the formidable edicts published by Charles V. However, the Lutheran propaganda, though a menace to the established church, had no quarrel with either the state or society. The first protestants were in no wise revolutionaries, and remained absolutely loyal to the emperor who sent them to the stake. But through the breach which they had made in traditional beliefs, anabaptism almost immediately flowed into the Low Countries.

Brought to Emden in 1529 by Melchior Hoffman, it spread at once through the northern provinces and speedily reached Brabant, Flanders and Limburg. The simplicity of anabaptist theology and its apoca-lyptic mysticism exercised an irresistible attraction on the minds of the common people. The new doctrine condemned the organization of society as the work of the evil one and aspired to destroy it. It claimed to found on the ruins of the existing social system the Heavenly City, where there was no room for inequality and injustice, and where love and charity would break down all social distinctions. How could such pro-mises fail to gain the enthusiastic adhesion of the swarms of poor labourers whose numbers, both in the towns and the country districts, were ever increasing owing to the new economic conditions? Its influence was similar to that of the lollards upon the weavers in the Middle Ages.

The illimitable hopes which anabaptism planted in the hearts of the people, the dazzling contrast which it drew, between the misery of their present condition and the blissful future in a world freed from the double oppression of church and state, put the patience and the resignation of the toiling masses to an excessively severe test. Hoffman certainly did not preach violence; but it was inevitable that his converts should have recourse to it sooner or later. In 1533 a prophet arose among the people in John Matthijs, a baker of Haarlem. He came to announce to the " just " and the " pure " the hour of vengeance, It was no longer enough to await patiently the Kingdom of God; it must be established by the sword. The wicked must be rooted out and the walls of the New Jerusalem must be cemented with their blood. **Away with priests!** But also, away with property, the army, law courts, and masters! From this time the religious question became also a social one. All the supporters of the established order, regardless of religious differences, banded themselves together against the anarchic mysticism of the anabaptists. The protestants hated them as much as the catholics. They were hunted down with the pitiless ferocity of blind fear. During the siege of Münster, where the chiefs of the movement had assembled to found the New Jerusalem, the soldiers of Mary of Hungary cut to pieces the bands who were marching to join their brethren. In the month of June 1535, a proclamation condemned all the anabaptists to death, even those who should abjure their errors.

The fall of Münster (June 25th, 1535) put an end to the revolutionary attempts of the anabaptists. The crisis had been too violent to recur again. Although the sect did not disappear, its tendencies were modified. It ceased to draw recruits from the lower orders. It gave birth to gentle and inoffensive communities of faithful souls who aimed at restoring primitive christianity on the basis of brotherly love and individual liberty without clergy or sacraments. Nevertheless it long continued under the ban of the state. No church has supplied so many victims to the heresy-hunters, and when the first Calvinists appeared in the Low Countries, they were at first confounded with the anabaptists, though they hated the anabaptists as fiercely as they hated the catholics.

Calvinism was no less revolutionary than anabaptism, but in a different way. Instead of attacking society, its aim was to destroy the church. Moreover the destruction of the church was sought only in order to set up a new church in its place. And this church, the instrument of God's law, conceived that part of its mission was to reconstruct the state in accordance with its own spirit, that is to say, it was to be submitted to the rule of the Calvinist church. Its ideal consisted in the subjection of the lay power to the authority of the church. The end to be attained was the theocratic state, such as the master, Calvin, had founded at Geneva. The gospel was to triumph despite even the prince, who was considered as nothing but a tyrant so long as he opposed the word of God. Thus the revolution let loose by the anabaptists against society was transferred by the Calvinists to the political arena. It appealed at once to all classes of the people. Its propaganda, bold, active and militant, soon won it adherents in the most diverse social spheres, from among the nobility, from among the capitalists from the lower middle class, and from the wage-earners.

It was, however, among the working class that Calvin's teaching spread most rapidly. The chief centres of its growth were to be found just where the great industries were supreme. It made the most rapid progress at Tournai, Valenciennes, Lille, Hondschoote and Armentières, around Oudenarde, in the ports of Holland and Zealand, and finally at Antwerp, the very centre of the economic life of the Low Countries. Above all, it triumphed where the worker was reduced to a precarious existence, and where his sufferings drove him to catch at every novelty. Discontent, the spirit of revolt, and the hope of bettering his lot, worked without exception in favour of Calvinism and thus the seed, sown in the hearts of the people by its ministers, grew into a hardy plant. A crowd of workmen, who had already broken with the traditional church under the influence of anabaptism, flung themselves impetuously upon the new doctrine. In proportion as the excitement grew, wastrels, vagabonds, and adventurers, in short, all the troublesome elements that are roused by any deep-reaching social change, threw their brute force on to the side of the new faith. In this way the greedy appetites of the mob swelled, while corrupting, the enthusiasm excited by the new gospel. Philip II, who succeeded Charles V in 1555, shewed little of his father's tact and his clumsiness soon excited a furious opposition. The higher nobility resented his policy of centralization. The emigration from the Netherlands of thousands of Calvinists fleeing from religious persecution brought about an industrial crisis. Other sources of trouble were the incompetent government of Margaret of Parma, the confederation of the great nobles against her, and the extravagance of their claims. All these circumstances suddenly brought on, in 1566, a decisive crisis. This was the rising of the iconoclasts. Beginning from the manufacturing districts of Hondschoote and Armentières, the movement spread from town to town, to the extreme limits of the Low Countries. The people thought that the moment had come for the destruction of the " idolatry of Rome." They burst into the churches, broke the statues, tore down the pictures. Thieves, who mingled with fanatics, greedily seized on the rich booty that religious fury put at their mercy.

Philip II. hastened to profit by the opportunity.

Ever since his accession he had steadily given way before the political opposition headed by Egmont and Orange. The outrage done to the church at length permitted him to take his revenge. From the summer of 1567 the duke of Alva, invested with unlimited power and commanding an army of picked soldiers, replaced the governor, Margaret of Parma, at Brussels. The punishment of the iconoclasts was not the new governor's only mission. The king had ordered him to extirpate heresy and impose a rigorous absolute government on the Low Countries. The ancient constitution of the provinces, respected by Charles V., was now trampled under foot. The duke governed alone without consulting the Council of State or calling the States General. As for the towns, what privileges and self-government still remained to them, were arbitrarily swept away. The constitution imposed on Ghent in 1540 became that of all the great communes. Citadels were constructed at Antwerp, at Valenciennes and Maestricht. In 1570 Alva thought that his work was completed. He had successfully defeated the army of William of Orange, beheaded the chief lords of the opposition and sent to the stake, the block or the gallows, hundreds of image-breakers, calvinists and other suspicious persons. He had re-established obedience by terror. He believed that a mere policeman would be sufficient to administer the country.

Alva's tyranny had exasperated the whole nation. The Spanish government, which had trampled under foot the liberties of all the provinces, was hardly less hateful to the catholic majority than to the protestant minority. A passive but unconquerable resistance

P

was aroused by taxes of the tenth and the twentieth penny, imitated from the Castilian *alcalabas,* which Alva claimed to impose on the provinces that they might henceforth pay for the maintenance of the troops who kept them in subjection. In the presence of their Spanish garrisons, the towns perceived that taking up arms would only end in useless massacres. They had recourse to a general strike. The artisans shut up their workshops; the salesmen deserted the market-place; all business was suspended and the terrible duke in the face of the dumb protest of a whole nation gave way to bursts of impotent fury.

II.

The Towns under Calvinist Government.

Such was the situation when on April 1st, 1572, a bold stroke threw the little town of Brielle into the power of the "beggars," as the rebels were called. Immediately, in all the neighbouring towns where the garrisons were away, the people rose, opened the gates to the liberators and turned out the magistrates. The calvinists took the lead in the movement. Relying on the lower classes, the fishermen and the throng of poor men, whom the new taxes had reduced to despair, they turned the political situation to their advantage. In a few weeks all the exiles who had been driven out of the provinces by the tyranny of Alva, all the protestants who had preferred banishment to renunciation of their faith, poured into Zealand. French Huguenots hastened to swell their ranks. Religious conviction, hatred of the papacy, hatred of Spain and finally, the reckless courage of men who had nothing to lose but life, made of the heterogeneous and cosmopolitan mob a redoubtable army if only a leader could be found for it. Such a leader was found in William of Nassau. He put himself at the head of the rebels. Like his following, he risked everything in the hope of gaining everything. With him in command chaos gave way to order. The mob lording it over the disorderly towns was reduced to discipline. Everything was subordinated to the necessities of defence. All men yielded to the clear-headed unswerving genius of William the Silent.

Despite this the southern provinces fell back under the power of Spain. During the heroic resistance which Holland and Zealand offered, first to Alva (1572—1573), and then to Requesens (1573—1576), the south made no effort to shake off the alien yoke. In proportion as the rebellion took on a character more and more calvinistic, the sympathy which it had at first elicited in Belgium, where the catholic element was much the stronger, gave place little by little to distrust. When, in 1576, after the unexpected death of the governor Requesens, the Council of State and the States General were charged with the provisional administration of the country, we find these bodies asserting their loyalty to king Philip and their determination not to tolerate any religion but catholicism, and displaying, still more clearly, their growing antipathy to the prince of Orange. The great nobles tried to exploit the situation so as to recover the ascendancy they had enjoyed under Margaret of Parma. Their policy was to restore to the country its old traditional constitution as it existed in the time of the dukes of Burgundy and Charles V.

It was then that the towns took the lead. An opposition, like that of the nobility, who continued to protest their loyalty to their lawful prince, no longer satisfied them. They demanded radical measures. The hatred roused by the Spanish government urged them to an open rupture with Philip II. The success of the resistance in Holland and Zealand excited their hopes of winning absolute freedom. Among the educated middle class, the political pamphlets, issued on the morrow of the massacre of St. Bartholomew, which definitely upheld the right of the people to depose a tyrant, were greedily devoured and applied against Philip. Then came, in 1576, the Pacification of Ghent, which established between the rebellious and the obedient provinces a defensive alliance, based upon respect for individual liberty of conscience. After this the calvinist propaganda grew more active than ever and, as before, attracted to it the masses which had been already stirred by it some years previously.

Soon religion and politics were inextricably mingled in Belgium as in Holland. Opposition to Spain involved at the same time adherence to the reformers, who profited by all the animosities that Philip had drawn upon himself. It was to no purpose that municipal magistrates, the members of the Council of State, the deputies of the States General, in short all the constituted authorities, remained catholic. Power had clearly slipped from their hands into those of the mob, which was subject both to the influence of the calvinistic ministers, and to that of the emissaries of the prince of Orange. The burghers of Brussels terrorized the States General which sat in their midst. All at once Ghent, excited by the example of the

capital, pushed matters to an extremity. Two dema-
gogues, relying on the calvinist party, seized the
government of the town. Thanks to the troops sent
by Orange to attack the citadel, to which the Spanish
garrison had fled for refuge, they established a purely
protestant government, persecuted the catholics and
opened conventicles, in which fanatical preachers
incited the people to overthrow idols and expel the
clergy. But to give this religious revolution some
appearance of legality, and at the same time to
emphasize its opposition to the monarchy, the constitution abolished by Charles V in 1540, was restored.
All the ancient privileges of the municipality were
again established. As in the Middle Ages, the commune was divided into three " members "; the *collace*
was called together; the crafts again entered into their
political rights, while the small towns and villages of
the castelry again fell under the power of Ghent.

This restoration of the mediæval system was mere
antiquarianism. The old institutions were no longer
workable because they no longer corresponded to the
actual condition of the population. Owing to the utter
ruin of the cloth trade, the "member" of the weavers
existed only in name, while the introduction of new
industries and the decline of the old ones, made the
revival of the fifty-two traditional crafts an anachronism. That, however, was of little importance.
Actually no one thought of reviving the old municipal
organization; its restoration was only a formality; the
underlying reality had nothing in common with it.
In fact, the government was carried on neither by the
crafts nor by the *collace,* but by the council of war,
a sort of committee of public safety in which sat the

calvinist leaders and the chief officers of the troops.
The government of the town was entirely military.
The spirit animating this government had nothing in
common with the old municipal spirit. Its aim was
the absolute triumph of calvinism, and it drew its
inspiration from the pastors, who ceaselessly fanned
its fanaticism against the catholic majority. Pro-
testantism became the persecuting instead of a persecuted body. Thanks to some regiments of soldiers
and to the support of the masses, calvinism got power
into its hands and abused it. At Brussels and at
Antwerp similar conditions produced like results.
There too " committees of the eighteen " had regular
troops at their disposal, and, under cover of the old
institutions, in reality exercised a dictatorship which
was half theocratic and half demagogic. In vain the
prince of Orange strove to recall the insane zealots to
reason ; in vain he urged upon them the need of
moderation, of the maintenance of liberty of conscience
and the supreme duty of uniting all their forces
against the common foe. Their ungoverned religious
passion now turned upon him. Ministers denounced
him from the pulpit as a papist. The prudence and
the caution, which his political genius imposed upon
them, were branded as treason and an outrage to the
divine majesty. In the eyes of the fanatical calvinists
who lorded it over the great towns, the national union
of the Netherlands no longer mattered. What they
wanted was a federal system of cantons as in Switzerland ; liberty for each great town to organize within its
walls the strict and exclusive observance of the "true
religion" and to impose it on to the neighbouring
countryside. It was of small account that the nobility,

exasperated by their fanaticism, returned to the king; and that the Walloon provinces, where the protestant host had not penetrated and where the calvinist minority was powerless, concluded peace with Farnese; nothing was done to remedy the situation. The towns remained irreconcilable until the day when, one after another, they were blockaded by the Spanish troops, and, finally opening their gates to the conquerors, suffered the fate that William of Orange had predicted.

CHAPTER XI.

THE TOWNS IN THE 17TH CENTURY.

I. Town Government in the United Provinces and Belgium.—II. The End of Democracy in the Bishopric of Liége.

I.

Town Government in the United Provinces and Belgium.

The re-establishment of the Spanish power over the Belgian provinces at the end of the 16th century brought about the definitive separation of the Low Countries into two distinct states. In the north the republic of the Seven United Provinces, which had heroically defended their religious faith and their political independence, soon reached an unprecedented economic prosperity, which was moreover equalled by the brilliance of its artistic and scientific development. The southern territories, brought back by force to catholicism and the Spanish monarchy, were involved in the decadence of Spain; their commerce and industry flagged, intellectual life was extinguished, and finally they were devastated by the great wars of the 17th century. Yet striking as was the contrast, there were certain resemblances between the two countries. Their institutions, either established or reformed according to the same principles during the Burgundian period, presented in the one case as in the other the same general characteristics. The government of the towns became in particular almost the same both in the north and in the south, and this similarity of development, amid such widely different circumstances, is enough to prove that the changes which took place in that government corresponded to causes deeply seated in the essential tendencies of Netherlandish social life. The prevalent system may be briefly described alike in the case of the flourishing cities of the north as well as in the languishing towns of the south, by calling it a return to the patriciate. After the revolutionary effervescence, which accompanied the introduction of calvinism, order was ultimately everywhere restored in the interest of the wealthy commercial class. Moreover, violent measures were not required to effect this result, either in the United Provinces or in the catholic Low Countries. Whether calvinism finally won or lost, the people who had risen in its support abandoned power almost of their own free will. Under William of Orange and under Alexander Farnese, in protestant and catholic districts alike, the administration of the towns was left to the magistrates and the ancient political prerogatives of the craft guilds were allowed to fall into disuse. In Holland the independence of " regents " in their relations with the burghers was formally recognized by an ordinance of 1581, and the same position was reached at Utrecht in 1586. From this time the population of the towns was deprived of all power of interference in local affairs. The council, "the law" of the town, recruited from among quite a small number of rich families, monopolized the policing and the jurisdiction of the municipality.   An aristocratic spirit, enjoining obedience to authority, took the place of the democratic spirit.   The Town Hall, that had for many years witnessed the excited and tumultuous assemblies of the commune, no longer opened its doors except to the magistrates and officials of the various administrative departments. The situation was the same in the Belgian towns. There too, municipal power was concentrated in the hands of the rich.   If it still sometimes happened that the crafts raised an agitation, a very modest shew of force was sufficient to reduce them to order.   Further, these demonstrations, for we can no longer use the word riots in this connection, came to an end after the first third of the 17th century.

So thoroughly was the political activity of the craft guilds extinguished, that little by little, either by regulations or simply by administrative action, the state or the *échevins* suppressed the last existing traces of the democratic organization of the 14th century. By the end of the first half of the century, even the memory of democratic government had disappeared. The ancient charters by which it had been ratified mouldered forgotten in the dust of the archives;[1] without being formally abolished, they had slowly fallen into disuse.   Subject to the united action of the state and economic change, the particularist policy of the towns had been constantly restrained since the Burgundian period.   After struggling vigorously for its existence, the town resigned itself to the inevitable. Thereupon the institutions which it upheld and by

1. At Brussels in 1698, the bombardment by Boufflers having blown open a tower where the communal archives were preserved, there were discovered the franchises granted to the "nations," the evidence of which had been concealed long before by the magistrates.

which it found expression, of necessity suffered the same fate. In the 17th century each town still constituted a legal unity, and, collectively, the towns still possessed the right of representing the third estate in the local and national assemblies to the exclusion of the country districts. Yet the towns were restrained in every way by the centralized monarchy. A system based on the nation as a whole took the place of a system based on the interests of the towns. The patrician magistrates were nominated by the central power which, moreover, controlled all departments of municipal administration. There only remained a few unimportant traces of their old system of commercial and industrial protection. The policing of the markets and the monopolies, which were still held by the crafts concerned with the food supply, alone remained to recall the past. But they survived simply as troublesome obstacles to progress, and involved, generally speaking, a heavy burden on the population.

If the towns were no longer absolute autocrats of the economic destinies of the Netherlands, they still had considerable power to influence them. Within their walls dwelt the capitalists and the large employers who were the mainspring of the industries, which were spreading more and more widely over the country districts. These same men supported, either as directors or as shareholders, the local commercial companies. The wealthy burghers thus became men of affairs, manufacturers, speculators, whose complex interests were entwined with the whole national life and ceased to be restricted to the narrow circle of the commune. And what is true of its economic aspect is true also of its political life. The rich merchant classes supplied the personnel of the administration and sat in the assemblies of the state. In the United Provinces their influence was scarcely counterbalanced by that of the Stadtholder. In the catholic Low Countries they possessed opportunities of making their power felt by means of their strong position at least equal to that of the clergy and the nobility in the provincial estates, the only representative institutions that survived amid the sluggishness of the national life.

This circumstance explains why the history of the aristocratic governments of the 17th century was different from that of the patriciate of the Middle Ages. In the Middle Ages each town constituted an independent political and economic whole and its government could be overthrown by a mere local revolution. To do away with the patrician government in the 17th century, nothing less than an upheaval of the whole state was required, for the state had absorbed the towns. Thus rebellion in the towns in more modern times was not a mere revolt against the commune, but against the national government. The scale of political life was magnified like that of economic life. The next time the democracy marched to attack authority, its ideas, its claims, its method of propaganda, and its fashion of fighting no longer recalled the commune of days gone by. Between modern revolutionaries and their forerunners the same disproportion of forces and the same lack of continuity can be seen, as existed between the capitalists of the Middle Ages and those whom the Renaissance had brought to fill their place.

II.

The End of Town Democracy in the Bishopric of Liége.

Democratic government maintained itself much longer in Liége than in the other towns of the Low Countries. It did not finally disappear till quite the end of the 17th century. But the reasons for its survival justify exactly what we have said of the cause of its fall in the rest of the country. Municipal government lived on to such an advanced age at Liége, because there the causes that brought about its down-fall elsewhere, were late in appearing.

After it had been annexed to the Burgundian state in the reign of Charles the Bold, the principality of Liége had regained its independence and its traditional institutions. According to the terms of the peace of Fexhe (1316), the government was divided between the bishop and the "wish of the country," that is to say the local estates. As a matter of fact, it was divided between the bishop and the "city" of Liége. Neither the clergy, represented solely by the chapter of the cathedral, nor the nobility, few in numbers and not very wealthy, could counterbalance the action of the third estate in the popular assemblies, and the third estate in its turn was entirely dominated by the delegates of the capital. The development of the collieries in the 14th century and then, after the coming of the Renaissance, the growth of the metal-working industry and the manufacture of arms, had made Liége one of the most active industrial centres of the Low Countries. Also by the end of the Middle

Ages, the other " good towns " of the bishopric had, little by little, lost their economic prosperity. The result was similar to the situation which prevailed in several parts of Germany. Face to face with its bishop, the city of Liége had entered upon a duel, the issue of which was to give the definitive supremacy to one or other of the two rivals. The city aimed at transforming itself into a free town, that is to say, into a municipal republic, and at shaking off the sovereignty of the prince. From the second half of the 15th century we can see its first efforts in this direction.

The bishops were of necessity obliged to look abroad for defence. The course they adopted against their city was that pursued by the Flemish towns against the dukes of Burgundy and their successors of the house of Hapsburg. The position in the bishopric of Liége was therefore exactly the reverse of that in the Low Countries. In the Netherlands generally the prince had at his disposal immense resources, and the principle of heredity sanctioned his power. In Liége, on the contrary, the bishop possessed only the revenues derived from his see. Further, his subjects were not bound to him by any strong bond, seeing that he was put over their country by reason of political or religious considerations absolutely independent of their local interests. Indeed the bishop often acted in a fashion contrary to the interests of the town when these clashed with his own family interests, or with the conditions of his appointment. Obviously he could not hold his own against the opposition of the commune save with the support which was given to him, first by the house of Burgundy, and afterwards

by the Spanish governors at Brussels. But the very
fact that his sovereign rights could only be maintained
by an alliance with a neighbouring power, suspected
of meditating the annexation of the country, filled his
people with constant distrust. The cause of the prince
seemed to be opposed to the popular cause, and the
efforts of the bishop to strengthen their position were
hampered by all sorts of obstacles.

On the other hand it may be noticed that the policy
of the towns in the bishopric of Liége did not run
upon the rocks encountered in Flanders. Instead of
several great towns, jealous of one another, the
bishopric only contained a single powerful commune,
its capital. Again the slow industrial development of
Liége allowed it to adapt itself easily to the new
economic conditions. Liége had not, like Bruges or
Ghent, to defend superannuated privileges and an
established position. In the industrial field the tendencies shewn in Liége suggest those at Antwerp in
the field of commerce. Liége threw open her doors
wide to foreigners, and she was not hampered either
by monopolies or by the privileges that the old cities
struggled to maintain to the public injury. Instead
of remaining stationary and clinging desperately to
antiquated privileges, its population steadily increased
and did not discover any need for industrial protection. We find, after close study, that Liége, from the
beginning of the 16th century, does not possess the
real economic system characteristic of the Middle
Ages. It was a great industrial centre working for
exportation, and attracting all the activity of the
principality. There is, therefore, nothing astonishing
in the desire the town felt to direct the policy of the

country and to confine the bishops to the simple discharge of their spiritual functions.

Such indeed was the end Liége set before itself in the long fight she maintained against the bishops. The crafts, which from 1603 had gained the right to nominate directly the *jurés* of the council and the two burgomasters, did not attempt, as in Flanders, to preserve their economic privileges. Their action was entirely political and their ideal openly republican. The long law suits they carried on in the courts of the empire, to get Liége recognized as a free town, in contempt of all historical truth, did not leave the least doubt about the nature of their designs. From the beginning of the 17th century, the conflict assumed an acute character in consequence of the intrigues of France and the United Provinces. A continued agitation was carried on against the Bavarian bishops, Ferdinand and Maximilian-Henry, who were the allies of Spain. The burghers divided into two parties : the *Chiroux* and the *Grignoux,* the Chiroux supporting the bishop, the Grignoux eagerly opposing him. Anarchy was rampant in public affairs. Electoral intrigues, corruption, and the continual interference of the resident envoys that France, the United Provinces and Spain maintained in the city, excited disturbances of increasing gravity. In vain the bishop disregarded the settlement of 1603. In vain the burgomaster, La Ruelle, one of the most popular chiefs of the opposition, was assassinated in 1637. From 1549 to 1684 five other burgomasters suffered on the scaffold.

Indeed it was not until that date, that bishop Maximilian-Henry of Bavaria succeeded in forcing on Liége a constitution which was to last till the era of

the French Revolution. France, which so far had
supported the commune, had just abandoned it in
favour of an alliance with the bishop, whose victory
was thereby assured. Political anarchy had left an
impossible situation in the city. The crafts, which
had only been able to keep their position owing to
the weakness of the bishop, found themselves powerless when his power was backed by that of the king
of France. They lost the political privileges which
they had so long retained. Thus, at Liége, as elsewhere, the struggle ended in the triumph of the state.
It must, however, be added that the democratic
institutions of Liége had had their day. The thirty-
two crafts, which nominated the council, had not been
able to organize a strong government in the town.
Gradually they had fallen under the leadership of a
group of agitators and intriguers. They had proved
incapable of overcoming the difficulties confronting
the state by reason of the rival ambitions of their
neighbours, France and Spain. As is commonly the
case with popular governments, they had sacrificed
everything to domestic politics; they did not understand that the king of France was absolutely indifferent
to their feelings and interests, and that he only concerned himself with them in order to maintain his
influence on the frontiers of the Seven United
Provinces. The refusal of the plenipotentiaries at the
congress of Nijmegen to admit the representatives of
Liége did not open their eyes, and it required the
catastrophe of 1684 to teach them, that, in the 17th
century, it was an anachronism and an impossibility to
make their own city the sole centre of their political
interests. Moreover no one was sorry when the

Q

government of the crafts failed. No one made the least attempt to restore it during the revolution at Liége at the end of the 18th century. New ideas had grown up, and it was the doctrine of the Rights of Man that then guided the attempt to establish a new social order.

INDEX

245